THE EYE
OF CHILDHOOD

'Tis the eye of childhood that fears a painted devil.

So said Lady Macbeth, pouring scorn on her husband Macbeth in Shakespeare's play. But who is to say if it is a painted devil, or a real one? Reality is what we make it, whether it is a child or an adult looking through the telescope.

Adults forget what it was like. Childhood is a different territory, with its own boundaries, its own hills and valleys, ravines and mountains. Seen from that enclosed landscape the adult world can appear baffling, infuriating, ridiculous, evil, or just plain terrifying. Not many of the childhoods in these stories could be described as happy ones, but then, as Frank McCourt said in his memoir of a childhood, *Angela's Ashes*: 'When I look back on my childhood I wonder how I survived at all. It was, of course, a miserable childhood: the happy childhood is hardly worth your while.'

But we begin with Jo, in whose young life there are no painted devils as yet; only a disconcerting departure from the established pattern of her experience . . .

OXFORD BOOKWORMS COLLECTION

Acknowledgements

The editors and publishers are grateful for permission to use the following copyright material:

'Killing Lizards' from *On the Yankee Station* by WILLIAM BOYD, published by Hamish Hamilton 1981, Penguin Books 1982. Copyright © William Boyd 1981, 1982. Reproduced by permission of the author c/o Rogers, Coleridge & White Ltd, 20 Powis Mews, London W11 1JN.

'The Runaway' from *Morley Callaghan Stories* by MORLEY CALLAGHAN © 1959. Reprinted by permission of Macmillan Canada.

'The End of the Party' from *Collected Short Stories* by GRAHAM GREENE, published by Penguin Books. Copyright © Graham Greene 1986. Reprinted by permission of David Higham Associates Ltd.

'Friends of Miss Reece' from *The Albatross and Other Stories* by SUSAN HILL. Copyright © Susan Hill 1970. Reprinted by permission of Richard Scott Simon Ltd.

'The Rocking-Horse Winner' by D. H. LAWRENCE from *The Collected Short Stories of D. H. Lawrence*. Reprinted by permission of Laurence Pollinger Ltd and the Estate of Frieda Lawrence Ravagli.

'Next Term, We'll Mash You' from *Pack of Cards* by PENELOPE LIVELY, published by Heinemann and Penguin Books 1986. Reprinted by permission of Murray Pollinger.

'Secrets' from *Secrets and Other Stories* by BERNARD MACLAVERTY, published 1979. Reprinted by permission of the author and The Blackstaff Press, Belfast.

'The Licence' by FRANK TUOHY from *The Collected Stories of Frank Tuohy*. Reprinted by permission of the Peters Fraser & Dunlop Group Ltd.

'Should Wizard Hit Mommy?' from *Pigeon Feathers and Other Stories* by JOHN UPDIKE. Copyright © 1959 by John Updike. Originally published in 'The New Yorker'. Reprinted by permission of Alfred A. Knopf Inc.

'The Open Window' by SAKI (H. H. Munro), first collected in *Beasts and Super-Beasts* 1914, was originally published by The Bodley Head, and appears by courtesy of the Estate of the author.

THE EYE
OF
CHILDHOOD

Short Stories

EDITED BY
John Escott
Jennifer Bassett

SERIES ADVISERS
H. G. Widdowson
Jennifer Bassett

OXFORD UNIVERSITY PRESS

OXFORD
UNIVERSITY PRESS

Great Clarendon Street, Oxford OX2 6DP

Oxford University Press is a department of the University of Oxford.
It furthers the University's objective of excellence in research, scholarship,
and education by publishing worldwide in

Oxford New York

Auckland Cape Town Dar es Salaam Hong Kong Karachi
Kuala Lumpur Madrid Melbourne Mexico City Nairobi
New Delhi Shanghai Taipei Toronto

With offices in

Argentina Austria Brazil Chile Czech Republic France Greece
Guatemala Hungary Italy Japan Poland Portugal Singapore
South Korea Switzerland Thailand Turkey Ukraine Vietnam

OXFORD and OXFORD ENGLISH are registered trade marks of
Oxford University Press in the UK and in certain other countries

© Oxford University Press 2000

The moral rights of the authors have been asserted

Database right Oxford University Press (maker)

First published 2000

12 14 16 18 20 19 17 15 13

ISBN 978 0 19 422813 8

Printed in China

Oxford Bookworms
~ Collection ~

Foreword

Texts of all kinds, including literary texts, are used as data for language teaching. They are designed or adapted and pressed into service to exemplify the language and provide practice in reading. These are commendable pedagogic purposes. They are not, however, what authors or readers of texts usually have in mind. The reason we read something is because we feel the writer has something of interest or significance to say and we only attend to the language to the extent that it helps us to understand what that might be. An important part of language learning is knowing how to adopt this normal reader role, how to use language to achieve meanings of significance to us, and so make texts our own.

The purpose of the *Oxford Bookworms Collection* is to encourage students of English to adopt this role. It offers samples of English language fiction, unabridged and unsimplified, which have been selected and presented to induce enjoyment, and to develop a sensitivity to the language through an appreciation of the literature. The intention is to stimulate students to find in fiction what Jane Austen found: 'the most thorough knowledge of human nature, the happiest delineation of its varieties, the liveliest effusions of wit and humour . . . conveyed to the world in the best chosen language.' *(Northanger Abbey)*

H. G. Widdowson
Series Adviser

Oxford Bookworms
~ Collection ~

None of the texts has been abridged or simplified in any way, but each volume contains notes and questions to help students in their understanding and appreciation.

Before each story
- a short biographical note on the author
- an introduction to the theme and characters of the story

After each story
- NOTES
  Some words and phrases in the texts are marked with an asterisk*, and explanations for these are given in the notes. The expressions selected are usually cultural references or archaic and dialect words unlikely to be found in dictionaries. Other difficult words are not explained. This is because to do so might be to focus attention too much on the analysis of particular meanings, and to disrupt the natural reading process. Students should be encouraged by their engagement with the story to infer general and relevant meaning from context.
- DISCUSSION
  These are questions on the story's theme and characters, designed to stimulate class discussion or to encourage the individual reader to think about the story from different points of view.
- LANGUAGE FOCUS
  Some of these questions and tasks direct the reader's attention to particular features of language use or style; others focus on specific meanings and their significance in the story.
- ACTIVITIES
  These are suggestions for creative writing activities, to encourage readers to explore or develop the themes of the story in various imaginative ways.
- QUESTIONS FOR DISCUSSION OR WRITING
  These are questions (sometimes under the heading 'Ideas for Comparison Activities') with ideas for discussion or writing which compare and contrast a number of stories in the volume.

CURRENT TITLES

From the Cradle to the Grave

Crime Never Pays

A Window on the Universe

The Eye of Childhood

And All for Love . . .

A Tangled Web

Contents

SHOULD WIZARD HIT MOMMY?

THE AUTHOR

John Updike was born in 1932 in Pennsylvania, in the USA.
He was educated at Harvard, and then went to the Ruskin
School of Art in Oxford, England. From 1955 to 1957 he was
on the staff of the *New Yorker*, and his first work appeared _ધપાવ_
in that magazine.

His novels include *The Centaur*, *Couples*, *The Coup*, and
The Witches of Eastwick, which was made into a major film.
His best-known novels are probably the 'Rabbit' series:
Rabbit Run, *Rabbit Redux*, *Rabbit is Rich*, and *Rabbit at
Rest*. He won the Pulitzer Prize for Fiction in 1982 for *Rabbit
is Rich*, and again in 1991 for *Rabbit at Rest*. As well as
novels, he has published many volumes of short stories,
books of poetry, collections of essays, and his memoirs.

THE STORY

Young children love to be told stories, especially at bedtime.
Often it is the same story, told over and over again, for the
familiar is comforting, reassuring. But should stories for
children always have happy endings, or should they
sometimes deal with the unpleasant realities of life? Should
they have a clear moral message? What should their purpose
be – to reassure, to instruct, to entertain, to stimulate the
imagination, to shock, to amuse?

Jo is four years old, with very firm ideas about what she
expects in her bedtime stories. Each one is a variation on a
familiar tale, and Jo likes to participate, knowing exactly
each character's designated role in the story. Her father Jack
strays from this well-trodden path at his peril . . .

SHOULD WIZARD HIT MOMMY?

In the evenings and for Saturday naps like today's, Jack told his daughter Jo a story out of his head. This custom, begun when she was two, was itself now nearly two years old, and his head felt empty. Each new story was a slight variation of a basic tale: a small creature, usually named Roger (Roger Fish, Roger Squirrel, Roger Chipmunk), had some problem and went with it to the wise old owl. The owl told him to go to the wizard, and the wizard performed a magic spell that solved the problem, demanding in payment a number of pennies greater than the number Roger Creature had but in the same breath directing the animal to a place where the extra pennies could be found. Then Roger was so happy he played many games with other creatures, and went home to his mother just in time to hear the train whistle that brought his daddy home from Boston. Jack described their supper, and the story was over. Working his way through this scheme was especially fatiguing on Saturday, because Jo never fell asleep in naps any more, and knowing this made the rite seem futile.

The little girl (not so little any more; the bumps her feet made under the covers were halfway down the bed, their big double bed that they let her be in for naps and when she was sick) had at last arranged herself, and from the way her fat face deep in the pillow shone in the sunlight sifting through the drawn shades, it did not seem fantastic that something magic would occur, and she would take her nap like an infant of two. Her brother, Bobby, was two, and already asleep with his bottle. Jack asked, 'Who shall the story be about today?'

'Roger . . .' Jo squeezed her eyes shut and smiled to be thinking she was thinking. Her eyes opened, her mother's blue. 'Skunk,' she said firmly.

A new animal; they must talk about skunks at nursery school. Having a fresh hero momentarily stirred Jack to creative enthusiasm. 'All right,' he said. 'Once upon a time, in the deep dark woods, there was a tiny little creature name of Roger Skunk. And he smelled very bad—'

'Yes,' Jo said.

'He smelled so bad none of the other little woodland creatures would play with him.' Jo looked at him solemnly; she hadn't foreseen this. 'Whenever he would go out to play,' Jack continued with zest, remembering certain humiliations of his own childhood, 'all of the other tiny animals would cry, "Uh-oh, here comes Roger Stinky Skunk," and they would run away, and Roger Skunk would stand there all alone, and two little round tears would fall from his eyes.' The corners of Jo's mouth drooped down and her lower lip bent forward as he traced with a forefinger along the side of her nose the course of one of Roger Skunk's tears.

'Won't he see the owl?' she asked in a high and faintly roughened voice.

Sitting on the bed beside her, Jack felt the covers tug as her legs switched tensely. He was pleased with this moment – he was telling her something true, something she must know – and had no wish to hurry on. But downstairs a chair scraped, and he realized he must get down to help Clare paint the living-room woodwork.

'Well, he walked along very sadly and came to a very big tree, and in the tiptop of the tree was an enormous wise old owl.'

'Good.'

' "Mr Owl," Roger Skunk said, "all the other little animals run away from me because I smell so bad." "So you do," the owl said. "Very, very bad." "What can I do?" Roger Skunk said, and he cried very hard.'

'The wizard, the wizard,' Jo shouted, and sat right up, and a Little Golden Book spilled from the bed.

'Now, Jo. Daddy's telling the story. Do you want to tell Daddy the story?'

'No. You me.'

'Then lie down and be sleepy.'

Her head relapsed onto the pillow and she said, 'Out of your head.'

'Well. The owl thought and thought. At last he said, "Why don't you go see the wizard?"'

'Daddy?'

'What?'

'Are magic spells real?' This was a new phase, just this last month, a reality phase. When he told her spiders eat bugs, she turned to her mother and asked, 'Do they *really*?' and when Clare told her God was in the sky and all around them, she turned to her father and insisted, with a sly yet eager smile, 'Is He *really*?'

'They're real in stories,' Jack answered curtly. She had made him miss a beat in the narrative. 'The owl said, "Go through the dark woods, under the apple trees, into the swamp, over the crick—"'

'What's a crick?'

'A little river. "Over the crick, and there will be the wizard's house." And that's the way Roger Skunk went, and pretty soon he came to a little white house, and he rapped on the door.' Jack rapped on the window sill, and under the covers Jo's tall figure clenched in an infantile thrill. 'And then a tiny little old man came out, with a long white beard and a pointed blue hat, and said, "Eh? Whatzis? Whatcher* want? You smell awful."' The wizard's voice was one of Jack's own favorite effects; he did it by scrunching up his face and somehow whining through his eyes, which felt for the interval rheumy. He felt being an old man suited him.

'"I know it," Roger Skunk said, "and all the little animals run away from me. The enormous wise owl said you could help me."

' "Eh? Well, maybe. Come on in. Don't git* too close." Now, inside, Jo, there were all these magic things, all jumbled together in a big dusty heap, because the wizard did not have any cleaning lady.'

'Why?'

'Why? Because he was a wizard, and a very old man.'

'Will he die?'

'No. Wizards don't die. Well, he rummaged around and found an old stick called a magic wand and asked Roger Skunk what he wanted to smell like. Roger thought and thought and said, "Roses." '

'Yes. Good,' Jo said smugly.

Jack fixed her with a trancelike gaze and chanted in the wizard's elderly irritable voice:

> ' "Abracadabry, hocus-poo*,
> Roger Skunk, how do you do,
> Roses, boses, pull an ear,
> Roger Skunk, you never fear:
> Bingo!" '

He paused as a rapt expression widened out from his daughter's nostrils, forcing her eyebrows up and her lower lip down in a wide noiseless grin, an expression in which Jack was startled to recognize his wife feigning pleasure at cocktail parties. 'And all of a sudden,' he whispered, 'the whole inside of the wizard's house was full of the smell of – roses! "Roses!" Roger Fish cried. And the wizard said, very cranky, "That'll be seven pennies." '

'Daddy.'

'What?'

'Roger Skunk. You said Roger Fish.'

'Yes. Skunk.'

'You said Roger Fish. Wasn't that silly?'

'Very silly of your stupid old daddy. Where was I? Well, you know about the pennies.'

'Say it.'

'O.K. Roger Skunk said, "But all I have is four pennies," and he began to cry.' Jo made the crying face again, but this time without a trace of sincerity. This annoyed Jack. Downstairs some more furniture rumbled. Clare shouldn't move heavy things; she was six months pregnant. It would be their third.

'So the wizard said, "Oh, very well. Go to the end of the lane and turn around three times and look down the magic well and there you will find three pennies. Hurry up." So Roger Skunk went to the end of .the lane and turned around three times and there in the magic well were three pennies! So he took them back to the wizard and was very happy and ran out into the woods and all the other little animals gathered around him because he smelled so good. And they played tag, baseball, football, basketball, lacrosse, hockey, soccer, and pick-up-sticks.'

'What's pick-up-sticks?'

'It's a game you play with sticks.'

'Like the wizard's magic wand?'

'Kind of. And they played games and laughed all afternoon and then it began to get dark and they all ran home to their mommies.'

Jo was starting to fuss with her hands and look out of the window, at the crack of day that showed under the shade. She thought the story was all over. Jack didn't like women when they took anything for granted; he liked them apprehensive, hanging on his words.

'Now, Jo, are you listening?'

'Yes.'

'Because this is very interesting. Roger Skunk's mommy said, "What's that awful smell?"'

'Wha-at?'

'And Roger Skunk said, "It's me, Mommy. I smell like roses." And she said, "Who made you smell like that?" And he said, "The wizard," and she said, "Well, of all the nerve. You come with me and we're going right back to that very awful wizard."'

Jo sat up, her hands dabbling in the air with genuine fright. 'But Daddy, then he said about the other little aminals* run away!' Her hands skittered off, into the underbrush.

'All right. He said, "But Mommy, all the other little animals run away," and she said, "I don't care. You smelled the way a little skunk should have and I'm going to take you right back to that wizard," and she took an umbrella and went back with Roger Skunk and hit that wizard right over the head.'

'No,' Jo said, and put her hand out to touch his lips, yet even in her agitation did not quite dare to stop the source of truth. Inspiration came to her. 'Then the wizard hit *her* on the head and did not change that little skunk back.'

'No,' he said. 'The wizard said "O.K." and Roger Skunk did not smell of roses any more. He smelled very bad again.'

'But the other little amum – *oh!* – amum—'

'Joanne. It's Daddy's story. Shall Daddy not tell you any more stories?' Her broad face looked at him through sifted light, astounded. 'This is what happened, then. Roger Skunk and his mommy went home and they heard *Woo-oo, woooo-oo* and it was the choo-choo* train bringing Daddy Skunk home from Boston. And they had lima beans, pork chops, celery, liver, mashed potatoes, and Pie-Oh-My for dessert. And when Roger Skunk was in bed Mommy Skunk came up and hugged him and said he smelled like her little baby skunk again and she loved him very much. And that's the end of the story.'

'But Daddy.'

'What?'

'Then did the other little ani-mals run away?'

'No, because eventually they got used to the way he was and did not mind it at all.'

'What's evenshiladee?'

'In a little while.'

'That was a stupid mommy.'

'It was *not*,' he said with rare emphasis, and believed, from her expression, that she realized he was defending his own mother to her, or something as odd. 'Now I want you to put your big heavy head in the pillow and have a good long nap.' He adjusted the shade so not even a crack of day showed, and tiptoed to the door, in the pretense that she was already asleep. But when he turned, she was crouching on top of the covers and staring at him. 'Hey. Get under the covers and fall faaast asleep. Bobby's asleep.'

She stood up and bounced gingerly on the springs. 'Daddy.'

'What?'

'Tomorrow, I want you to tell me the story that that wizard took that magic wand and hit that mommy' – her plump arms chopped fiercely – 'right over the head.'

'No. That's not the story. The point is that the little skunk loved his mommy more than he loved aaalll the other little animals and she knew what was right.'

'No. Tomorrow you say he hit that mommy. Do it.' She kicked her legs up and sat down on the bed with a great heave and complaint of springs, as she had done hundreds of times before, except that this time she did not laugh. 'Say it, Daddy.'

'Well, we'll see. Now at least have a rest. Stay on the bed. You're a good girl.'

He closed the door and went downstairs. Clare had spread the newspapers and opened the paint can and, wearing an old shirt of his on top of her maternity smock, was stroking the chair rail with a dipped brush. Above him footsteps vibrated and he called, 'Joanne. Shall I come up there and spank you?' The footsteps hesitated.

'That was a long story,' Clare said.

'The poor kid,' he answered, and with utter weariness watched his wife labor. The woodwork, a cage of moldings and rails and baseboards all around them, was half old tan and half new ivory and he felt caught in an ugly middle position, and though he as well felt his wife's presence in the cage with him, he did not want to speak with her, work with her, touch her, anything.

Notes

Whatzis, Whatcher want (p12)

  phonetic spellings of spoken forms of 'What's this?' and 'What do you want?'

git (p13)

  a spoken variant of 'get'

abracadabry, hocus poo (p13)

  words and phrases like these are said as 'magic' words by magicians at the moment of performing a magic trick

aminals (p15)

  animals (young children sometimes transpose letters in words when speaking)

choo-choo (p15)

  the noise made by a train, and a word sometimes used by young children to mean a train

Discussion

1 Jack refuses to alter the ending of his story simply to please his daughter. Do you think he was right to do that? What would *you* have done?

2 If there are any 'messages' in Jack's story to Jo, they might be that children should love their parents more than their friends, and that a mother 'knows what is right'. Do you think these are appropriate messages for a four-year-old child?

3 Why do you think Jo was so determined that the wizard should fight back against the interference by Roger Skunk's mommy? Is the author suggesting that Jo does not like her own mother, or that she is a natural rebel and is beginning to challenge all parental authority, or that it was simply her way of objecting to the change in the story's routine?

4 'Jack didn't like women when they took anything for granted; he liked them apprehensive, hanging on his words.' What does that suggest to you about Jack's character?

5 How did you interpret the last paragraph of the story? Do you think Jack's weariness, his sense of being in a cage, is the result of his argument with Jo, because he feels her beginning to escape from his dominance? Or, in Jack's sudden feeling of alienation from his wife, is the author suggesting something more sinister, a hint perhaps of fault lines in the relationship, threatening the stability of the family unit?

Language Focus

1 What do these expressions mean, as used in the story? Find them in the text and rephrase them in your own words.

in the same breath   (p10)
Out of your head   (p12)
made him miss a beat in the narrative   (p12)
scrunching up his face   (p12)
when they took anything for granted   (p14)
hanging on his words   (p14)
Well, of all the nerve   (p15)
they got used to the way he was   (p15)
with a . . . complaint of springs   (p16)

2 When Jo asks her father if magic spells are real, Jack replies, *'They're real in stories.'*

What do you think of this answer? Is there anything contradictory in it? Is it an appropriate explanation to give to a child of Jo's age? Think of other ways of explaining this idea in simple language.

Activities

1 Imagine that Jack does add a new ending to please his daughter. What would happen between the wizard, Roger Skunk, and Roger Skunk's mommy? Write the new ending for the story as though you were telling it to Jo yourself.

2 What elements do you think should ideally be included in stories for children under five years of age? What elements should ideally be excluded? For example, are the following desirable elements or not?
- a familiar environment such as a family home or a school
- a strong authority figure
- punishment for wrongdoing
- a character who is a source of wisdom or comfort
- horrible monsters
- violence

Make two lists, adding further ideas of your own. Then use your lists to write a paragraph of guidance for writers of children's stories.

The End of the Party

The Author

Graham Greene was born in 1904. Educated at Oxford University, he then worked for various newspapers, was an intelligence agent in the Second World War, and frequently travelled in remote and dangerous places. He wrote novels, short stories, plays, and travel books. Among his lighter novels, which Greene called 'entertainments', are *Stamboul Train*, *A Gun for Sale*, *Our Man in Havana*, and *The Third Man*, which was made into a famous film. Greene himself preferred his other novels, which reflect his intense interest in religious and moral issues (he was a Roman Catholic convert). These powerful and sombre novels include *Brighton Rock*, *The Power and the Glory*, *The End of the Affair*, *The Heart of the Matter*, *A Burnt-out Case*, and *The Human Factor*. Greene died in 1991.

The Story

Fear is an emotion that can be aroused by almost anything. 'I will show you fear in a handful of dust,' wrote T. S. Eliot in his famous poem *The Waste Land*. Fear is not easy to explain, and often even harder to admit to – especially for children, who might have to face both the dismissive incomprehension of adults and the mocking scorn of other children.

Francis and his twin brother, Peter, are going to a children's party, where they will be obliged to play noisy games with the other children. Francis, unable to explain to anyone his paralysing fear of the dark, anticipates with secret horror the worst of these games – hide and seek, *in the dark*. Peter, instinctively aware of his twin's inarticulate terror, tries hard to protect him . . .

The End of the Party

Peter Morton woke with a start to face the first light. Rain tapped against the glass. It was January the fifth.

He looked across a table on which a night-light* had guttered into a pool of water, at the other bed. Francis Morton was still asleep, and Peter lay down again with his eyes on his brother. It amused him to imagine it was himself whom he watched, the same hair, the same eyes, the same lips and line of cheek. But the thought palled, and the mind went back to the fact which lent the day importance. It was the fifth of January. He could hardly believe a year had passed since Mrs Henne-Falcon had given her last children's party.

Francis turned suddenly upon his back and threw an arm across his face, blocking his mouth. Peter's heart began to beat fast, not with pleasure now but with uneasiness. He sat up and called across the table, 'Wake up.' Francis's shoulders shook and he waved a clenched fist in the air, but his eyes remained closed. To Peter Morton the whole room seemed to darken, and he had the impression of a great bird swooping. He cried again, 'Wake up,' and once more there was silver light and the touch of rain on the windows. Francis rubbed his eyes. 'Did you call out?' he asked.

'You are having a bad dream,' Peter said. Already experience had taught him how far their minds reflected each other. But he was the elder, by a matter of minutes, and that brief extra interval of light, while his brother still struggled in pain and darkness, had given him self-reliance and an instinct of protection towards the other who was afraid of so many things.

'I dreamed that I was dead,' Francis said.

'What was it like?' Peter asked.

'I can't remember,' Francis said.

'You dreamed of a big bird.'

'Did I?'

The two lay silent in bed facing each other, the same green eyes, the same nose tilting at the tip, the same firm lips, and the same premature modelling of the chin. The fifth of January, Peter thought again, his mind drifting idly from the image of cakes to the prizes which might be won. Egg-and-spoon races, spearing apples in basins of water, blind man's buff*.

'I don't want to go,' Francis said suddenly. 'I suppose Joyce will be there . . . Mabel Warren.' Hateful to him, the thought of a party shared with those two. They were older than he. Joyce was eleven and Mabel Warren thirteen. The long pigtails* swung superciliously to a masculine stride. Their sex humiliated him, as they watched him fumble with his egg, from under lowered scornful lids. And last year . . . he turned his face away from Peter, his cheeks scarlet.

'What's the matter?' Peter asked.

'Oh, nothing. I don't think I'm well. I've got a cold. I oughtn't to go to the party.'

Peter was puzzled. 'But Francis, is it a bad cold?'

'It will be a bad cold if I go to the party. Perhaps I shall die.'

'Then you mustn't go,' Peter said, prepared to solve all difficulties with one plain sentence, and Francis let his nerves relax, ready to leave everything to Peter. But though he was grateful he did not turn his face towards his brother. His cheeks still bore the badge of a shameful memory, of the game of hide and seek last year in the darkened house, and of how he had screamed when Mabel Warren put her hand suddenly upon his arm. He had not heard her coming. Girls were like that. Their shoes never squeaked. No boards whined under the tread. They slunk like cats on padded claws.

When the nurse* came in with hot water Francis lay tranquil leaving everything to Peter.

Peter said, 'Nurse, Francis has got a cold.'

The tall starched woman laid the towels across the cans and said, without turning, 'The washing won't be back till tomorrow. You must lend him some of your handkerchiefs.'

'But, Nurse,' Peter asked, 'hadn't he better stay in bed?'

'We'll take him for a good walk this morning,' the nurse said. 'Wind'll blow away the germs. Get up now, both of you,' and she closed the door behind her.

'I'm sorry,' Peter said. 'Why don't you just stay in bed? I'll tell mother you felt too ill to get up.' But rebellion against destiny was not in Francis's power. If he stayed in bed they would come up and tap his chest and put a thermometer in his mouth and look at his tongue, and they would discover he was malingering. It was true he felt ill, a sick empty sensation in his stomach and a rapidly beating heart, but he knew the cause was only fear, fear of the party, fear of being made to hide by himself in the dark, uncompanioned by Peter and with no night-light to make a blessed breach.

'No, I'll get up,' he said, and then with sudden desperation, 'But I won't go to Mrs Henne-Falcon's party. I swear on the Bible I won't.' Now surely all would be well, he thought. God would not allow him to break so solemn an oath. He would show him a way. There was all the morning before him and all the afternoon until four o'clock. No need to worry when the grass was still crisp with the early frost. Anything might happen. He might cut himself or break his leg or really catch a bad cold. God would manage somehow.

He had such confidence in God that when at breakfast his mother said, 'I hear you have a cold, Francis,' he made light of it. 'We should have heard more about it,' his mother said with irony, 'if there was not a party this evening,' and Francis smiled, amazed and daunted by her ignorance of him. His happiness would have lasted longer if, out for a walk that morning, he had not met Joyce. He was alone with his nurse, for Peter had leave to finish a rabbit-hutch in the woodshed. If Peter had been there he would have cared less; the nurse was Peter's nurse also, but now it was as though she were employed only for his sake, because he could not be trusted to go for a walk alone. Joyce was only two years older and she was by herself.

She came striding towards them, pigtails flapping. She glanced scornfully at Francis and spoke with ostentation to the nurse. 'Hello, Nurse. Are you bringing Francis to the party this evening? Mabel and I are coming.' And she was off again down the street in the direction of Mabel Warren's home, consciously alone and self-sufficient in the long empty road. 'Such a nice girl,' the nurse said. But Francis was silent, feeling again the jump-jump of his heart, realizing how soon the hour of the party would arrive. God had done nothing for him, and the minutes flew.

They flew too quickly to plan any evasion, or even to prepare his heart for the coming ordeal. Panic nearly overcame him when, all unready, he found himself standing on the doorstep, with coat-collar turned up against a cold wind, and the nurse's electric torch making a short trail through the darkness. Behind him were the lights of the hall and the sound of a servant laying the table for dinner, which his mother and father would eat alone. He was nearly overcome by the desire to run back into the house and call out to his mother that he would not go to the party, that he dared not go. They could not make him go. He could almost hear himself saying those final words, breaking down for ever the barrier of ignorance which saved his mind from his parents' knowledge. 'I'm afraid of going. I won't go. I daren't go. They'll make me hide in the dark, and I'm afraid of the dark. I'll scream and scream and scream.' He could see the expression of amazement on his mother's face, and then the cold confidence of a grown-up's retort.

'Don't be silly. You must go. We've accepted Mrs Henne-Falcon's invitation.' But they couldn't make him go; hesitating on the doorstep while the nurse's feet crunched across the frost-covered grass to the gate, he knew that. He would answer: 'You can say I'm ill. I won't go. I'm afraid of the dark.' And his mother: 'Don't be silly. You know there's nothing to be afraid of in the dark.' But he knew the falsity of that reasoning; he knew how they taught also that there was nothing to fear in death, and how fearfully they avoided the idea of it. But they couldn't make him go to the party. 'I'll scream. I'll scream.'

'Francis, come along.' He heard the nurse's voice across the dimly phosphorescent lawn and saw the yellow circle of her torch wheel from tree to shrub. 'I'm coming,' he called with despair; he couldn't bring himself to lay bare his last secrets and end reserve between his mother and himself, for there was still in the last resort a further appeal possible to Mrs Henne-Falcon. He comforted himself with that, as he advanced steadily across the hall, very small, towards her enormous bulk. His heart beat unevenly, but he had control now over his voice, as he said with meticulous accent, 'Good evening, Mrs Henne-Falcon. It was very good of you to ask me to your party.' With his strained face lifted towards the curve of her breasts, and his polite set speech, he was like an old withered man. As a twin he was in many ways an only child. To address Peter was to speak to his own image in a mirror, an image a little altered by a flaw in the glass, so as to throw back less a likeness of what he was than of what he wished to be, what he would be without his unreasoning fear of darkness, footsteps of strangers, the flight of bats in dusk-filled gardens.

'Sweet child,' said Mrs Henne-Falcon absent-mindedly, before, with a wave of her arms, as though the children were a flock of chickens, she whirled them into her set programme of entertainments: egg-and-spoon races, three-legged races, the spearing of apples, games which held for Francis nothing worse than humiliation. And in the frequent intervals when nothing was required of him and he could stand alone in corners as far removed as possible from Mabel Warren's scornful gaze, he was able to plan how he might avoid the approaching terror of the dark. He knew there was nothing to fear until after tea, and not until he was sitting down in a pool of yellow radiance cast by the ten candles on Colin Henne-Falcon's birthday cake did he become fully conscious of the imminence of what he feared. He heard Joyce's high voice down the table, 'After tea we are going to play hide and seek in the dark.'

'Oh, no,' Peter said, watching Francis's troubled face, 'don't let's. We play that every year.'

'But it's in the programme,' cried Mabel Warren. 'I saw it myself. I looked over Mrs Henne-Falcon's shoulder. Five o'clock tea. A quarter to six to half past, hide and seek in the dark. It's all written down in the programme.'

Peter did not argue, for if hide and seek had been inserted in Mrs Henne-Falcon's programme, nothing which he could say would avert it. He asked for another piece of birthday cake and sipped his tea slowly. Perhaps it might be possible to delay the game for a quarter of an hour, allow Francis at least a few extra minutes to form a plan, but even in that Peter failed, for children were already leaving the table in twos and threes. It was his third failure, and again he saw a great bird darken his brother's face with its wings. But he upbraided himself silently for his folly, and finished his cake encouraged by the memory of that adult refrain, 'There's nothing to fear in the dark.' The last to leave the table, the brothers came together to the hall to meet the mustering and impatient eyes of Mrs Henne-Falcon.

'And now,' she said, 'we will play hide and seek in the dark.'

Peter watched his brother and saw the lips tighten. Francis, he knew, had feared this moment from the beginning of the party, had tried to meet it with courage and had abandoned the attempt. He must have prayed for cunning to evade the game, which was now welcomed with cries of excitement by all the other children. 'Oh, do let's.' 'We must pick sides.' 'Is any of the house out of bounds?' 'Where shall home* be?'

'I think,' said Francis Morton, approaching Mrs Henne-Falcon, his eyes focused unwaveringly on her exuberant breasts, 'it will be no use my playing. My nurse will be calling for me very soon.'

'Oh, but your nurse can wait, Francis,' said Mrs Henne-Falcon, while she clapped her hands together to summon to her side a few children who were already straying up the wide staircase to upper floors. 'Your mother will never mind.'

That had been the limit of Francis's cunning. He had refused to believe that so well prepared an excuse could fail. All that he could say now, still in the precise tone which other children hated, thinking it a symbol of conceit, was, 'I think I had better not play.' He stood motionless, retaining, though afraid, unmoved features. But the knowledge of his terror, or the reflection of the terror itself, reached his brother's brain. For the moment, Peter Morton could have cried aloud with the fear of bright lights going out, leaving him alone in an island of dark surrounded by the gentle lappings of strange footsteps. Then he remembered that the fear was not his own, but his brother's. He said impulsively to Mrs Henne-Falcon, 'Please, I don't think Francis should play. The dark makes him jump so.' They were the wrong words. Six children began to sing, 'Cowardy cowardy custard*,' turning torturing faces with the vacancy of wide sunflowers towards Francis Morton.

Without looking at his brother, Francis said, 'Of course I'll play. I'm not afraid, I only thought . . .' But he was already forgotten by his human tormentors. The children scrambled round Mrs Henne-Falcon, their shrill voices pecking at her with questions and suggestions. 'Yes, anywhere in the house. We will turn out all the lights. Yes, you can hide in the cupboards. You must stay hidden as long as you can. There will be no home*.'

Peter stood apart, ashamed of the clumsy manner in which he

had tried to help his brother. Now he could feel, creeping in at the corners of his brain, all Francis's resentment of his championing. Several children ran upstairs, and the lights on the top floor went out. Darkness came down like the wings of a bat and settled on the landing. Others began to put out the lights at the edge of the hall, till the children were all gathered in the central radiance of the chandelier, while the bats squatted round on hooded wings and waited for that, too, to be extinguished.

'You and Francis are on the hiding side,' a tall girl said, and then the light was gone, and the carpet wavered under his feet with the sibilance of footfalls, like small cold draughts, creeping away into corners.

'Where's Francis?' he wondered. 'If I join him he'll be less frightened of all these sounds.' 'These sounds' were the casing of silence: the squeak of a loose board, the cautious closing of a cupboard door, the whine of a finger drawn along polished wood.

Peter stood in the centre of the dark deserted floor, not listening but waiting for the idea of his brother's whereabouts to enter his brain. But Francis crouched with fingers on his ears, eyes uselessly closed, mind numbed against impressions, and only a sense of strain could cross the gap of dark. Then a voice called 'Coming', and as though his brother's self-possession had been shattered by the sudden cry, Peter Morton jumped with his fear. But it was not his own fear. What in his brother was a burning panic was in him an altruistic emotion that left the reason unimpaired. 'Where, if I were Francis, should I hide?' And because he was, if not Francis himself, at least a mirror to him, the answer was immediate. 'Between the oak bookcase on the left of the study door, and the leather settee.' Between the twins there could be no jargon of telepathy. They had been together in the womb, and they could not be parted.

Peter Morton tiptoed towards Francis's hiding-place. Occasionally a board rattled, and because he feared to be caught by one of the soft questers through the dark, he bent and untied his laces. A tag struck the floor and the metallic sound set a host of cautious feet moving in his direction. But by that time he was in his stockings and would have laughed inwardly at the pursuit had not the noise of someone stumbling on his abandoned shoes made his heart trip. No more boards revealed Peter Morton's progress. On stockinged feet he moved silently and unerringly towards his object. Instinct told him he was near the wall, and, extending a hand, he laid the fingers across his brother's face.

Francis did not cry out, but the leap of his own heart revealed to Peter a proportion of Francis's terror. 'It's all right,' he whispered, feeling down the squatting figure until he captured a clenched hand. 'It's only me. I'll stay with you.' And grasping the other tightly, he listened to the cascade of whispers his utterance had caused to fall. A hand touched the book-case close to Peter's head and he was aware of how Francis's fear continued in spite of his presence. It was less intense, more bearable, he hoped, but it remained. He knew that it was his brother's fear and not his own that he experienced. The dark to him was only an absence of light; the groping hand that of a familiar child. Patiently he waited to be found.

He did not speak again, for between Francis and himself was the most intimate communion. By way of joined hands thought could flow more swiftly than lips could shape themselves round words. He could experience the whole progress of his brother's emotion, from the leap of panic at the unexpected contact to the steady pulse of fear, which now went on and on with the regularity of a heartbeat. Peter Morton thought with intensity, 'I am here. You needn't be afraid. The lights will go on again soon. That rustle, that movement is nothing to fear. Only Joyce, only Mabel Warren.' He bombarded the drooping form with thoughts of safety, but he was conscious that the fear continued. 'They are beginning to whisper together. They are tired of looking for us. The lights will go on soon.

We shall have won. Don't be afraid. That was someone on the stairs. I believe it's Mrs Henne-Falcon. Listen. They are feeling for the lights.' Feet moving on a carpet, hands brushing a wall, a curtain pulled apart, a clicking handle, the opening of a cupboard door. In the case above their heads a loose book shifted under a touch. 'Only Joyce, only Mabel Warren, only Mrs Henne-Falcon,' a crescendo of reassuring thought before the chandelier burst, like a fruit-tree, into bloom.

The voices of the children rose shrilly into the radiance. 'Where's Peter?' 'Have you looked upstairs?' 'Where's Francis?' but they were silenced again by Mrs Henne-Falcon's scream. But she was not the first to notice Francis Morton's stillness, where he had collapsed against the wall at the touch of his brother's hand. Peter continued to hold the clenched fingers in an arid and puzzled grief. It was not merely that his brother was dead. His brain, too young to realize the full paradox, wondered with an obscure self-pity why it was that the pulse of his brother's fear went on and on, when Francis was now where he had always been told there was no more terror and no more darkness.

NOTES

night-light (p22)

a small, slow-burning candle, used in children's bedrooms at night in case they wake up and are frightened by the dark

blind man's buff (p23)

a children's game in which a player whose eyes are covered tries to catch and identify the other players

pigtails (p23)

long hair plaited or tied together in two lengths at the back of the head

nurse (p23)

a short form of *nursemaid*, a woman or girl employed to look after babies or small children in their own homes

home, no home (p28)

in children's games, such as hide and seek or games of chase, 'home' is the agreed place where you are safe from being chased or caught

cowardy cowardy custard (p28)

a taunt used by children when they think someone is scared (custard is yellow, and yellow is the colour associated with cowardice)

DISCUSSION

1 In your opinion, who, if anyone, is to blame for Francis's death? Explain in what ways these characters might have unwittingly contributed to the tragedy: the nurse, the children's mother, Mrs Henne-Falcon, the other children, Peter – perhaps even Francis himself.

2 Do you think that Peter, with the natural resilience of children, will eventually recover from this dreadful experience, or will he suffer from a lifelong feeling of guilt? Why might he feel guilty? And what do you think the author is suggesting in the last paragraph, by saying that 'the pulse of his brother's fear went on and on'?

3 This story was written in 1929, a time in Britain when it was thought that children should be 'seen and not heard'. Do you think that children today are more actively encouraged to express their feelings? If so, is this a good thing or a bad thing? Explain why you think this.

LANGUAGE FOCUS

1 Find these expressions in the story and then rephrase them in your own words.

   his cheeks still bore the badge of a shameful memory   (p23)
   the tall starched woman   (p23)
   with no night-light to make a blessed breach   (p24)
   he made light of it   (p24)
   breaking down for ever the barrier of ignorance   (p25)
   he couldn't bring himself to lay bare his last secrets   (p26)

2 The author uses several images that reinforce the feelings of fear and isolation that Francis, and Peter, experience:

   the impression of a great bird swooping
   like cats on padded claws
   an island of dark
   torturing faces with the vacancy of wide sunflowers
   darkness came down like the wings of a bat

   How do these images work in the story? Do you find them effective?

ACTIVITIES

1 Imagine this story was set in a time when children felt freer to express their feelings. Francis is embarrassed but not afraid to tell his parents about his fear of the dark. Write a conversation between him and his mother when he tries to explain why he doesn't want to go to the party.

2 Poor Francis is not very imaginative when it comes to inventing excuses, first at home, and then at the party:

   'I've got a cold. I oughtn't to go to the party.'
   'I think it will be no use my playing. My nurse will be calling for me very soon.'

   Suggest some more cunning and effective excuses he could have invented on both occasions.

3 Some days later perhaps Mrs Henne-Falcon writes to Mrs Morton. Write the letter for her, expressing deep sympathy at Francis's death but also making it clear that she does not regard herself as responsible in any way. There might even be a hint of reproach at Mrs Morton's failure to mention poor Francis's sensibility.

KILLING LIZARDS

THE AUTHOR

William Boyd was born in 1952 in Accra, Ghana, and was brought up there and in Nigeria. He was educated at the universities of Nice, Glasgow, and Oxford, and from 1980 to 1983 he was a lecturer in English Literature at St Hilda's College, Oxford. His first novel, *A Good Man in Africa*, won a Whitbread Literary Award, and later novels have also won literary prizes. His titles include *An Ice-Cream War, Stars and Bars, The New Confessions, Brazzaville Beach*, and *The Blue Afternoon*. Eight of his screenplays have been filmed, including *A Good Man in Africa*, based on his first novel.

The story in this book is taken from his collection of short stories entitled *On the Yankee Station*.

THE STORY

'There is always one moment in childhood,' wrote Graham Greene in his novel *The Power and the Glory*, 'when the door opens and lets the future in.' But the future can come in many shapes and forms. It might come as an unexpected opportunity, a new friendship, an unwelcome experience. Or it might come as knowledge – the kind of knowledge that confers power on the owner of it.

As a rule, children do not have much power. Gavin, who is twelve, yearns for his mother's interest and attention, but cannot get it. He spends much of his Easter holidays out with his friends under the hot African sun, killing lizards with stones from a catapult. That is exercising power, of a kind, and Gavin derives uneasy pleasure from it. Then one day he acquires a piece of knowledge that holds the shape of his future . . .

KILLING LIZARDS

Gavin squatted beside Israel, the cook's teenage son, on the narrow verandah of the servants' quarters. Israel was making Gavin a new catapult. He bound the thick, rubber thongs to the wooden Y with string, tying the final knot tight and nipping off the loose ends with his teeth. Gavin took the proffered catapult and tried a practice shot. He fired at a small grove of banana trees by the kitchen garden. The pebble thunked into a fibrous bole with reassuring force.

'Great!' Gavin said admiringly, then 'hey!' as Israel snatched the catapult back. He dangled the weapon alluringly out of Gavin's reach and grinned as the small twelve-year-old boy leapt angrily for it.

'Cig'rette. Give me cig'rette,' Israel demanded, laughing in his high wheezy way.

'Oh, all right,' Gavin grudgingly replied, handing over the packet he had stolen from his mother's handbag the day before. Israel promptly lit one up and confidently puffed smoke up into the washed-out blue of the African sky.

Gavin walked back up the garden to the house. He was a thin dark boy with a slightly pinched face and unusually thick eyebrows that made his face seem older than it was. He went through the kitchen and into the cool spacious living room with its rugs and tiled floor, where two roof fans energetically beat the hot afternoon air into motion.

The room was empty and Gavin walked along the verandah past his bedroom and that of his older sister. His sister, Amanda, was at boarding school in England; Gavin was going to join her there next year. He used to like his sister but since her fifteenth birthday she had changed. When she had come out on holiday last Christmas she had hardly played with him at all. She was bored with him; she preferred going shopping with her mother. A conspiracy of sorts seemed to have sprung up between the women of the family from which Gavin and his father were excluded.

When he thought of his sister now, he felt that he hated her. Sometimes he wished the plane that was bringing her out to Africa would crash and she would be killed. Then there would only be Gavin, he would be the only child. As he passed her bedroom he was reminded of his fantasy and despite himself he paused, thinking about it again, trying to imagine what life would be like – how it would be different. As he did so the other dream began to edge itself into his mind, like an insistent hand signalling at the back of a classroom drawing attention to itself. He had this dream quite a lot these days and it made him feel peculiar: he knew it was bad, a wrong thing to do, and sometimes he forced himself not to think about it. But it never worked, for it always came faltering back with its strange imaginative allure, and he would find himself lost in it, savouring its pleasures, indulging in its sweet illicit sensations.

It was a variation on the theme of his sister's death, but this time it also included his father. His father and sister had died in a car crash and Gavin had to break the news to his mother. As she sobbed with grief she clung to him for support. Gavin would soothe her, stroking her hair as he'd seen done on TV in England, whispering words of comfort.

In the dream Gavin's mother never remarried, and she and Gavin returned to England to live. People would look at them in the street, the tall elegant widow in black and her son, growing tall and more mature himself, being brave and good by her side. People around them seemed to whisper, 'I don't know what she would have done without him' and 'Yes, he's been a marvel' and 'They're so close now'.

Gavin shook his head, blushing guiltily. He didn't hate his father

– he just got angry with him sometimes – and it made him feel bad and upset that he kept on imagining him dead. But the dream insistently repeated itself, and it continued to expand; the narrative furnished itself with more and more precise details; the funeral scene was added, the cottage Gavin and his mother took near Canterbury, the plans they made for the school holidays. It grew steadily more real and credible – it was like discovering a new world – but as it did, so Gavin found himself more and more frustrated and oppressed by the truth, more dissatisfied with the way things were.

Gavin slowly pushed open the door of his parents' bedroom. Sometimes he knocked, but his mother had laughed and told him not to be silly. Still, he was cautious as he had once been horribly embarrassed to find them both asleep, naked and sprawled on the rumpled double bed. But today he knew his father was at work in his chemistry lab. Only his mother would be having a siesta.

But Gavin's mother was sitting in front of her dressing table brushing her short but thick reddish auburn hair. She was wearing only a black bra and pants that contrasted strongly with the pale freckly tan of her firm body. A cigarette burned in an ashtray. She brushed methodically and absentmindedly, her shining hair crackling under the brush. She seemed quite unaware of Gavin standing behind her, looking on. Then he coughed.

'Yes, darling, what is it?' she said without looking round.

Gavin sensed rather than appreciated that his mother was a beautiful woman. He did not realize that she was prevented from achieving it fully by a sulky turn to her lips and a hardness in her pale eyes. She stood up and stretched languidly, walking barefooted over to the wardrobe where she selected a cotton dress.

'Where are you going?' Gavin asked without thinking.

'Rehearsal, dear. For the play,' his mother replied.

'Oh. Well, I'm going out too.' He left it at that. Just to see if she'd say anything this time, but she seemed not to have heard. So he added, 'I'm going with Laurence and David. To kill lizards.'

'Yes, darling,' his mother said, intently examining the dress she had chosen. 'Do try not to touch the lizards, they're nasty things, there's a good boy.' She held the dress up in front of her and looked at her reflection critically in the mirror. She laid the dress on the bed, sat down again and began to apply some lipstick. Gavin looked at her rich red hair and the curve of her spine in her creamy back, broken by the dark strap of her bra, and the three moles on the curve of her haunch where it was tautened by the elastic of her pants. Gavin swallowed. His mother's presence in his life loomed like a huge wall at whose foot his needs cowered like beggars at a city gate. He wished she bothered about him more, did things with him as she did with Amanda. He felt strange and uneasy about her, proud and uncomfortable. He had been pleased last Saturday when she took him to the pool in town, but then she had worn a small bikini and the Syrian men round the bar had stared at her. David's mother always wore a swimsuit of a prickly material with stiff bones in it. When he went out of the room she was brushing her hair again and he didn't bother to say goodbye.

Gavin walked down the road. He was wearing a striped T-shirt, white shorts and Clarks* sandals without socks. The early afternoon sun beat down on his head and the heat vibrated up from the tarmac. On either side of him were the low senior-staff bungalows, shadowy beneath their wide eaves, and which seemed to be pressed down into the earth as if the blazing sun bore down with intolerable weight. The coruscating scarlet dazzle of flamboyant trees that lined the road danced spottily in his eyes.

The university campus was a large one but Gavin had come to know it intimately in the two years since his parents had moved to Africa. In Canterbury his father had only been a lecturer but here he was a professor in the Chemistry Department. Gavin loved to go down to the labs with their curious ammoniacal smells, brilliant fluids and mad-scientist constructions of phials, test-tubes and rubber pipes. He thought he might pay his father a surprise visit that afternoon as their lizard hunt should take them in that direction.

Gavin and his two friends had been shooting lizards with their catapults for the three weeks of the Easter holidays and had so far accounted for one hundred and forty-three. They killed mainly the male and female of one species that seemed to populate every group of boulders or area of concrete in the country. The lizards were large, sometimes growing to eighteen inches in length. The females were slightly smaller than the males and were a dirty speckled khaki colour. The males were more resplendent, with brilliant orange-red heads, pale grey bodies and black-barred feet and tails. They did no one any harm; just basked in the sun doing a curious bobbing press-up motion. At first they were ludicrously easy to kill. The boys could creep up to within three or four feet and with one well-placed stone reduce the basking complacent lizard to a writhing knot, its feet clawing at a buckled spine or shattered head. A slight guilt had soon grown up among the boys and they accordingly convinced themselves that the lizards were pests and that, rather like rats, they spread diseases.

But the lizards, like any threatened species, grew wise to the hunters and now scurried off at the merest hint of approach, and the boys had to range wider and wider through the campus to find zones where the word had not spread and where the lizards still clung unconcernedly to walls, like dozing sunbathers unaware of the looming thunderclouds.

Gavin met his friends at the pre-arranged corner. Today they were heading for the university staff's preparatory school at a far edge of the campus. There was an expansive outcrop of boulders there with a sizeable lizard community that they had been evaluating for some time, and this afternoon they planned a blitz.

They walked down the road firing stones at trees and clumps of bushes. Gavin teased Laurence about his bandy legs and then joined forces with him to mock David about his spots and his hugely fat sister until he threatened to go home. Gavin felt tense and malicious, and lied easily to them about how he had fashioned his own catapult, which was far superior to their clumsier home-made efforts. He was glad when they rounded a corner and came in sight of the long simple buildings of the chemistry labs.

'Let's go and see my Dad,' he suggested.

Gavin's father was marking exam papers in an empty lab when the three boys arrived. He was tall and thin with sparse black hair brushed across his balding head. Gavin possessed his similar tentative smile. They chatted for a while, then Gavin's father showed them some frozen nitrogen. He picked a red hibiscus bloom off a hedge outside and dipped it in the container of fuming liquid. Then he dropped the flower on the floor and it shattered to pieces like fine china.

'Where are you off to?' he asked as the boys made ready to leave.

'Down to the school to get lizards,' Gavin replied.

'There's a monster one down there,' said David. 'I've seen it.'

'I hope you don't leave them lying around,' Gavin's father said. 'Things rot in this sun very quickly.'

'It's okay,' Gavin affirmed brightly. 'The hawks soon get them.'

Gavin's father looked thoughtful. 'What's your mother doing?' he asked his son. 'Left her on her own, have you?'

'Israel's there,' Gavin replied sullenly. 'But anyway she's going to her play rehearsal or something. Drama, drama, you know.'

'Today? Are you sure?' his father asked, seemingly surprised.

'That's what she said. Bye, Dad, see you tonight.'

The school lay on a small plateau overlooking a teak forest and the jungle that stretched away beyond it. The outcrop of rocks was poised on the edge of the plateau and it ran down in pale pinkish slabs to the beginning of the teak trees.

The boys killed four female lizards almost at once but the others had rushed into crevices and stayed there. Gavin caught a glimpse of a large red-head as it scuttled off and the three of them pelted the deep niche it hid in and prodded at it with sticks, but it was just not coming out.

Then Gavin and Laurence thought they saw a fruit bat in a palm tree, but David couldn't see it and soon lost interest. They patrolled the deserted school buildings for a while and then hung, bat-like themselves, on the Jungle-Jim* in the playground. David, who had perched on the top, heard the sound of a car as it negotiated a bumpy rutted track that led into the jungle and which ran for a while along the base of the plateau. He soon saw a Volkswagen van lurching along. A man was driving and a woman sat beside him.

'Hey, Gavin,' David said without thinking. 'Isn't that your mother?'

Gavin climbed quickly up beside him and looked.

'No,' he said. 'Nope*. Definitely.'

They resumed their play but the implication hung in the air like a threat, despite their suddenly earnest jocularity. In the unspoken way in which these things arrange themselves, David and Laurence soon announced that they had to go home. Gavin said that he would stay on a bit. He wanted to see if he could get that big lizard.

Laurence and David wandered off with many a backward shouted message about where they would meet tomorrow and what they would do. Then Gavin clambered about half-heartedly on the Jungle-Jim before he walked down the slope to the track which he followed into the teak forest. There was still heat in the afternoon sun and the trees and bushes looked tired from a day's exposure. The big soup-plate leaves of the teak trees hung limply in the damp dusty atmosphere.

Gavin heard his mother's laugh before he saw the van. He moved off the track and followed the curve of a bend until he saw the van through the leaves. It was pulled up on the other side of the mud road. The large sliding door was thrown back and Gavin could see that the bunk bed inside had been folded down. His mother was sitting on the edge of the bunk, laughing. A man without a shirt was struggling to zip up her dress. She laughed again, showing her teeth and throwing back her head, joyously shaking her thick red hair. Gavin knew the man: he was called Ian Swan and sometimes came to the house. He had a neat black beard and curling black hair all over his chest.

Gavin stood motionless behind the thick screen of leaves and watched his mother and the man. He knew at once what they had been doing. He watched them caper and kiss and laugh. Finally Gavin's mother tugged herself free and scrambled round the van and into the front seat. Gavin saw a pair of sunglasses drop from her open handbag. She didn't notice they had fallen. Swan put on his shirt and joined her in the front of the van.

As they backed and turned the van Gavin held his breath in an agony of tension in case they should run over the glasses. When they had gone he stood for a while before walking over and picking up the sunglasses. They were quite cheap; Gavin remembered she had bought them last leave in England. They were favourites. They had pale blue lenses and candy-pink frames. He held them carefully in the palm of his hand as if he were holding an injured bird.

MUMMY . . .

As he walked down the track to the school the numbness, the blank camera stare that had descended on him the moment he had heard his mother's high laugh, began to dissipate. A slow tingling charge of triumph and elation began to infuse his body.

OH, MUMMY, I THINK . . .

He looked again at the sunglasses in his palm. Things would change now. Nothing would be the same after this secret. It seemed to him now as if he were carrying a ticking bomb.

OH, MUMMY, I THINK I'VE FOUND YOUR SUNGLASSES.

The lowering sun was striking the flat rocks of the outcrop full on and Gavin could feel the heat through the soles of his sandals as he walked up the slope. Then, ahead, facing away from him, he saw the lizard. It was catching the last warmth of the day, red head methodically bobbing, sleek torso and long tail motionless. Carefully Gavin set down the glasses and took his catapult and a pebble from his pocket. Stupid lizard, he thought, sunbathing, head bobbing like that, you never know who's around. He drew a bead* on it, cautiously easing the thick rubber back to full stretch until his rigid left arm began to quiver from the tension.

He imagined the stone breaking the lizard's back, a pink welling tear in the pale scaly skin. The curious slow-motion way the mortally wounded creatures keeled over, sometimes a single leg twitching crazily like a spinning rear wheel on an upended crashed car.

The lizard basked on, unaware.

Gavin eased off the tension. Holding his breath with the effort, heart thumping in his ears. He stood for a few seconds letting himself calm down. His mother would be home now, he should have enough time before his father returned. He picked up the sunglasses and backed softly away and around leaving the lizard undisturbed. Then, with his eyes alight and gleaming beneath his oddly heavy brows, he set off steadily for home.

NOTES

Clarks (p39)

the trade name of a British shoe manufacturer, particularly well-known for children's shoes and sandals

Jungle-Jim (p42)

a climbing frame found in children's playgrounds

nope (p42)

(informal) exclamation used to say 'no'

bead (to draw a bead on) (p44)

to take aim at

DISCUSSION

1 What do you think the following suggested about Gavin's character?
   • the incident with Israel, the catapult, and the cigarettes
   • Gavin's fantasy about the death of his father and sister
   • his mockery of his friends' bandy legs and spots
   • his denial to David that it was his mother in the van

2 At the end of the story Gavin is on the point of shooting the large male lizard, but at the last moment he resists the urge to kill it and walks away. What interpretation can you put on this? Is the author suggesting that Gavin suddenly feels sympathy for the lizard, or something else?

3 If an adult were to use information about a secret affair in the way that Gavin might use it, this would probably be called blackmail. Does Gavin's mother seem the sort of personality that will submit to blackmail? How do you think she is likely to react? How do you think she *should* react?

4 In his book *The Interpretation of Dreams* Sigmund Freud, the famous psychologist, said:

'Children are completely egoistic; they feel their needs intensely and strive ruthlessly to satisfy them.'

Do you think that Gavin's behaviour in this story supports this theory? Are there other explanations for Gavin's behaviour? If so, what might they be?

LANGUAGE FOCUS

1   The author uses quite a striking image to describe how Gavin feels about
    his mother:

    *His mother's presence in his life loomed like a huge wall at whose foot
    his needs cowered like beggars at a city gate.*

    Try rephrasing this idea in your own words, using straightforward
    language to describe emotions. Which version is longer, yours or the
    original? Which do you think is clearer, or more effective? Why?

2   Towards the end of the story the author uses this image about Gavin
    holding the sunglasses:

    . . . as if he were holding an injured bird

    and a second image a little later:

    . . . as if he were carrying a ticking bomb.

    What do these two images represent? Describe in your own words
    Gavin's two emotional states, and the probable transition between them.

ACTIVITIES

1   What do you think Gavin will actually say to his mother when he gets
    home? Will he be explicit, or just drop hints? How will his mother react?
    Write their conversation, beginning with

    'Oh, Mummy, I think I've found your sunglasses.'

2   Is the story really about killing lizards? Why do you think the author
    chose this title? Is it an appropriate one? Would any of these titles be
    more, or less, appropriate? Why?

    The Sunglasses   The Catapult
    A Mortal Wound   The Easter Holidays

    Now think of three or four more titles, and explain why you think they
    would be appropriate for the story.

FRIENDS OF MISS REECE

THE AUTHOR

Susan Hill was born in Scarborough, Yorkshire, in 1942. She was educated at grammar schools there and in Coventry, and studied at King's College, London. She is a novelist, playwright, broadcaster, and critic. A frequent theme of her fiction is loneliness, about which she writes with delicacy and compassion. She also writes about children with great sensitivity, and *I'm the King of the Castle*, probably her best-known book, reverberates with the terrors of childhood. Other titles include *A Change for the Better, In the Springtime of the Year, The Bird of Night, A Bit of Singing and Dancing, The Woman in Black* (a ghost story), and *Listening to the Orchestra and Other Stories*. The story in this volume was taken from her collection *The Albatross and Other Stories*.

THE STORY

Busy parents often 'park' their children while they get on with their jobs or their social lives. Children parked in this way, with childminders or relatives, have to cope as best they can. It might be a safe and friendly place, or a place full of lurking terrors and painted dragons – perhaps even real ones.

At the Cedars Lawn Nursing Home the Matron is the boy's aunt, and the boy is regularly parked there when his parents go away. Sickness and death are everyday occurrences at the Home, and the boy is not afraid of them. Indeed, his best friend is Miss Reece, who lies in bed unable to move or speak or do anything for herself. But the boy would much rather sit quietly and patiently in Miss Reece's room than have anything to do with the terrifying Nurse Wetherby . . .

FRIENDS OF MISS REECE

'You're in the way,' Wetherby said, but quietly, hissing under her breath, in case Matron, who was also the boy's Aunt, should come in through the door.

'Nuisance . . . as if there weren't enough.'

She bent down and jabbed at the coals with a black poker, so that they burst hotly open like poppy pods, showering sparks for seeds. He watched her covertly, out of the sides of his eyes, feeling ashamed of being so disliked. The warmth from the fire came up into his face.

'You can drink your milk on the hearth stool, you won't get under everyone's feet,' his Aunt Spencer had said. But she was kind, beneath the sharp way of talking. He had always known her.

'*Which* room was I born in?'

'Number Six, next to the old nursery, down the corridor from Reece.'

It was familiar as a rhyme. When he asked, she answered, automatically, hanging in and out of the swing doors with trays and pans and white enamel jugs of steaming water, always using the same words.

'Number Six, next to the old nursery, down the corridor from Reece.'

It was his mother who refused to comfort him in this way.

'*Which* room was I born in?'

'Oh, don't be silly, do try and remember, do stop asking the same questions, haven't I *told* you . . .'

Wetherby was dumping fresh coal on to the fire, in great chunks, darkening it. He felt the warmth go off his face, a sudden shadow. Wetherby held the starched white apron flat against her body, with her left hand, out of the way of the fire. The door swung in and out again, water glasses chinked on a loaded tray. One of the bells rang. He looked up at the little, glass-fronted box. There were rows of numbers, and rows of little scarlet flaps. When somebody rang their bell, the flap dropped down and up, down and up, down and up, under the number of their room. Six, he thought, let it be six. He closed his eyes, and opened them again. But it was not six, it was nine. Nobody ever rang from six, when he was here.

'Number Six, next to the old nursery, down the corridor from Reece.'

But Reece never rang her bell, either.

'Never wants anything,' Aunt Spencer had said. Yet Wetherby still hated her, still grumbled, just out of earshot of the Matron, about how much trouble she was given, by Reece.

He tipped the mug of cooling milk up to his face and allowed a very little to slide into his mouth. He did not want to finish it, Wetherby would notice. 'Upstairs with *you*, then, that's one thing out of the way, get along.'

Wetherby had always been here, in the Cedars Lawn Nursing Home, just as Reece had always been here, in Number Seven. He hated Wetherby, and he was a friend of Reece. '*Miss* Reece,' his mother made him say. And worried, vaguely, from time to time, about whether it did any harm to him, going so often to see her. But she supposed not.

He thought of how terrible it would be, if he were always in Number Seven, like Miss Reece, and always looked after and fed and woken and put to sleep and washed and chided, by Wetherby.

'*Nurse* Wetherby, to you . . .'

Once, he thought that the very first face he had ever seen had been that of Wetherby, it was the thing he could remember quite clearly, from the day of his birth, in Number Six.

'What did I look like?'

'A good, healthy baby,' said his Aunt Spencer, holding a white china feeding cup to the light, looking for a crack.

'*Red*,' Wetherby had told him, coming behind him and whispering, on the dark stairs. 'Red and ugly, that's what. You squalled.'

Her top teeth were very large, and yellow, with even gaps, and they stuck out below her lip, like a bow-window. He moved away quickly.

The milk was thickish, and sweet. He held it in his mouth and swirled his tongue around inside, comforted.

'We are going out until very late. It will be much nicer for you to sleep at the nursing home,' his mother had said. 'It will be a treat.'

He had looked away and out of the window, on to the garden, where the last of the melting snow lay, grubby as the stained linen that came down to Aunt Spencer's washroom in a hand-operated lift.

He would have said, I don't want to, I want to stay here, I don't like sleeping there all night, because of Wetherby. Once, he had half-spoken.

'*Nurse* Wetherby, to you, and you are very silly about her.'

'She's ugly.'

'Not everybody can be beautiful.'

'Her teeth are all yellow.'

'That is a nasty, *personal* remark, polite little boys do not say things like that.'

'She . . .'

But he could not have told. He kept his mind turned from the thought of the upstairs landings of the Cedars Lawn Nursing Home, and the attic where he must sleep, in the room next to Wetherby.

'Are you going to a ball?'

'No, dear.'

'To a dinner?'

For they were always putting on new clothes and getting into the warm car and driving off somewhere. The names of the people

whose houses they visited were familiar as those of the streets and
squares around which he walked, every afternoon, with the girl
Shirley, who was paid to take him out, by the hour.

'Are you going to the Mayor's Banquet, then?'

'Oh, don't be *silly*, that is in the spring. It is November now.'

'*Where* are you going?'

'To play bridge with Mr and Mrs Templeton. There, now.'

He knew that bridge was a game played with cards, sitting at
tables, yet whenever he heard the word, there was the same picture
in his mind, of the bridge over the lake in Beecher's Park, and the
railway bridge, and all the other bridges he had ever seen. He saw
the people, too, his mother and father, and the Templetons and the
Hoylakes and the Askew-Fishers, all rushing about on the bridges,
playing some kind of elegant tag, in their evening clothes.

'Why do I have to go to Aunt Spencer's? Why can't I stay at home
and be sat with?'

'Because I have told you, we shall be very late and it is altogether
more convenient, that is all. Now, eat up your carrots, please.'

There was only a dribble of milk left at the bottom of the mug.
He looked down into it and thought about his mother, in the palely
floating chiffon dress. The Templetons owned the Park Royal Hotel,
facing the Esplanade. It had a monkey puzzle tree, thick and dark
as felt, in the garden.

'Just *playing* with that,' Wetherby said venomously, and leaned
over, pushing her face close down towards him, to see the thin, liquid
layer in the blue mug. He smelled her starched cotton material in
the warmth from the fire, and the breath coming out from behind
her yellow teeth, like the thick, stale fumes of tea.

Aunt Spencer banged through the swing doors, with Night Sister
behind her, calling out that Eleven had been sick over the side of
the bed and down on to the floor. He heard about it, and was
unmoved, it seemed to him that the whole of adult life was about

these things, the sickness and temperatures and bowels and dying, of the patients in the nursing home. He was not afraid. He had always come here.

'*Bed* . . .' said Aunt Spencer suddenly, but when he looked up, he felt safe, knowing her concern for him, behind the bustling about and the care of so many patients. He had been the last child born at the Cedars Lawn Home, before they 'gave up maternity'. In the evenings, she had nursed him, beside the fire in her private sitting-room, warding off the recognition of her own growing old.

'Bed . . .'

He got up from the hearth stool.

'*Which* room was I born in?'

'Number Six, next to the old nursery, down the corridor from Reece.'

He paused at the kitchen door, satisfied. 'I could go and see her.'

'Who, Reece? No. Wetherby's gone to put her on the commode.'

'But I could just wait and then say good night to her.'

'She doesn't want visitors at this time of night.'

'It's only . . .' He looked up at the clock, but his memory failed him again, he still could not work out what the hands said, unless it were very straightforward, midday or six o'clock.

His father said, 'He is very *stupid* over this matter of telling the time,' and stared down at him, leaning forward a little. 'I hope he is not going to be stupid in many other respects.'

The fire was beginning to spurt through the new coals, now, he did not want to leave it, and the warmth and light and smells of the kitchen, for the iron-framed bed, five flights of stairs up in the dark attics. Aunt Spencer said, 'I'm going up to Eleven now, I'll come and see to you as well.'

She pushed open the swing door and he followed, looking at the stiff folds of her matron's cap, streaming behind her, and the black matron's shoes, and thick, black stockings, over stout legs. He felt better, now that she was to supervise his undressing and washing and the saying of prayers. He was not going to be left to Wetherby.

Outside the door of Six, he hesitated, staring at the magic number, in gold on the brown paint, feeling the importance of it.

'Don't dawdle,' Aunt Spencer said, beginning to be out of breath. 'We're short-staffed tonight and Twelve is dying, I haven't time to wait about for you.'

He glanced down the short corridor that led to Number Seven.

'You can see Reece in the morning.'

They began to climb the next, steep flight.

Nurse Wetherby, red and puffy about the face, banged the tray on the kitchen table. He looked up and then down again, quickly, stirring his spoon through the porridge.

'Nothing but a filthy, dirty mess,' Wetherby said, under her breath, 'things slopped everywhere.'

He flushed with alarm, and looked at the table around his plate anxiously, and down the front of his Fair Isle* jumper. But there was nothing, it was not him. Reece, he thought, Miss Reece.

'It's getting worse . . . slopping everything about . . . she's not fit to live.' The words came in spurts, from different parts of the kitchen, as Wetherby moved about. He knew that she was not talking to him.

Outside the window, he could see the sky, leaden with the new snow to come. He took another spoonful of sugar and tipped it slowly over the porridge, watching the brown grains spill and then sink into the soft mess, melting and leaving little stains. Aunt Spencer was upstairs with Nurse O'Keefe, laying out Number Twelve. He wondered what time his mother might come for him.

'*Dawdler*, you're as bad as that Reece, messing your food about, look at you. Huggitt's waiting to clear, I suppose you know.' He stiffened. It had been quite dark when she had woken him, coming into the attic. And then her thick fingers, fumbling with his pyjamas. He thought, when my mother comes, I shall tell her, or else I shall tell Aunt Spencer, and nobody will make me sleep here again. But he knew that he would say nothing, would not know the words to use. And he was afraid of Wetherby.

The door swung open. 'I thought you wanted to go and see Reece,' said Aunt Spencer.

Getting down from the table, he asked who had been Number Twelve. Aunt Spencer's arms were full of rubber hot water bottles, taken out, morning-cold, from the beds.

'Mr Perrott, poor old soul.' She turned to Wetherby. 'There's a brother-in-law, apparently,' she said, 'that's all. Never been here, you see, not interested. I shall have to ring. The undertaker's coming at three.'

He went out of the kitchen, and slowly up the first, linoleum-covered flight of stairs. After that, the polished wood began, and the ruby-red carpet, trodden by the shoes of the nurses and the doctors and the visitors of patients in Cedars Lawn. He thought about the dead Mr Perrott, in Number Twelve. Once he had been in to see him, but nothing was said, Mr Perrott had been asleep. He had been slightly relieved. There was always the one, bad moment, when they sent him to visit some new patient in a strange room. 'Go and cheer up Nine . . . Fifteen . . . Two . . . give the poor soul a bit of company, go on.' And he tapped upon the brown doors and pushed them open and went inside, and did not know what terrible things he might see.

Mr Perrott had been shrivelled, his skin and hair were the same, yellowish white. His mouth had been slightly open as he breathed. Twelve was the smallest room, facing on to the side of St Martin's Church. He had waited for a moment, politely, but Mr Perrott had not woken.

In the nursing home kitchen, Aunt Spencer had cut slice after slice of bread and said, 'Cancer', in passing, to his mother.

Now, Mr Perrott was dead.

He came to the door of Number Seven. Reece. She had been here when he was born – *before* he was born. There were those, like Mr Perrott, who came for a time and died and were replaced, and those, like Miss Reece, who stayed here forever. He knocked, but out of courtesy, because there would be no answer, and then opened the door.

'Rolling in money,' Wetherby said, 'everything it can buy. It means nothing to them, that family of hers, nothing at all.' For Miss Reece had the largest and most expensive room at the front of the Cedars Lawn Nursing Home, Miss Reece's bed overlooked the garden, and some of the furniture belonged to her family – the Sheraton* dressing-table at which she would never sit, and the Persian carpet and the armchairs for visitors, and the large picture over the mantelpiece. Miss Reece lay in the high bed, and her rich family paid, the sister and the two married brothers, and an elderly aunt, and once a week, on Sunday afternoons, they visited her, by turns. They arrived in chauffeured cars, wearing coats with fur collars and doing their duty, eating tea and being bored.

He walked around the screen and crossed the Persian carpet and stood beside the high bed. It took a long time for Miss Reece to move her head on the pillow, so that she ceased to gaze out of the window, and could focus upon him, instead. He waited. Reece, about whom Wetherby always complained, rich Miss Reece, with the straight grey hair and very soft skin and the tremor in head and body, hands and legs. 'Parkinson's*', Aunt Spencer had said once.

He saw the recognition of him, in the slight widening of her pale eyes. On the gold, quilted counterpane, her hands lay and shook. He said, 'I've just had my breakfast. I stayed here the night because my mother and father went out. They went to play bridge at the Park Royal Hotel.'

Once, Miss Reece had been able to nod, but now, he realized that he could no longer tell the difference between the nod of interest, and understanding, that was meant for him, and the helpless nodding which went on all the time.

'Did you have porridge as well? I had porridge.'

Like some small, individual animal, with a life of its own, the left hand of Miss Reece twitched slightly on the counterpane. The half-moons were sketched, white as chalk, on the oval nails.

'For Christmas, I'm going to have a puppy. It's going to be a spaniel. I could bring it to see you, couldn't I? You'd like that.'

The shaking continued.

He had thought that Reece was old, the oldest person in the world. She had been in her bed at the Cedars Lawn Nursing Home for eleven years. But when he had asked Aunt Spencer, she had said no, no, Reece wasn't old at all, was young, was not yet fifty, and that was the tragedy. She had had, Aunt Spencer said, 'no life'.

Now, he waited beside the bed, as the bell from St Martin's Church began to toll the hour. Eventually, Miss Reece would speak. He knew what she would say. It was always the same. He stood, rubbing the sole of his left sandal over the surface of his right, trying to be patient, for he must not say the words for her, must not be impolite. 'She isn't soft in the head,' Aunt Spencer had said. 'You needn't think that, just because her speech has gone. She's all there. You must show a decent respect no matter what.'

Only Wetherby muttered and grumbled, day after day, clashing the breakfast trays and the lunch trays and the trays with the visitors' teas, the jugs and bowls and bedpans, only Wetherby said, out of earshot of the Matron, that Reece was not fit to live.

He watched the small, flabby mouth begin to quiver, saw the tongue fumbling about wetly between palates, trying to grasp and form the words. There was a dribble of dried egg on one side of her chin. 'Messes,' Wetherby said, 'messes and dribbles her food like a baby. It's getting worse and worse. I know, I have to put up with it, nobody else, I can see the way she's going. Not fit to live.'

He wondered why Wetherby was a nurse, and then supposed that she could do nothing else, would not fit into any other world. He had watched her, shovelling spoonful after spoonful of liquid mess into Miss Reece's helpless mouth and never giving her enough time, making noises of impatience and irritation. But once, she had gone out of the room to answer a persistent bell, leaving the cup, and then, he had fetched a stool and stood upon it to reach the bed, and, very slowly and carefully, he had begun to put the food into Miss Reece's mouth. She had managed, there had been no dribble. But it had taken a long time. He dared not say anything to Wetherby. There would be the nights when he must sleep here, upstairs in the attic.

In the end, the words came. He understood them only because they were always the same.

'Would you like a sweet?'

It might have been some language spoken by one of a race whose mouths were shaped unlike human mouths, or else the noise of some animal, slurred and uncontrolled. He thought of what it must be like, to know the right words inside your head, to hear them there, and not to be able to bring them out, thought of words going around and around, all tangled together like washing inside a machine, trapped.

He said, 'Yes, I would. Thank you very much,' and waited again, for the hand to creep forwards, a little, over the gold counterpane, the forefinger to twitch, pointing as best it might, in the direction of the Sheraton dressing-table.

The box was made of tin, with a pattern painted on to it, to look like the stitchings of needlepoint*, roses and leaves on a black ground. Where the lid opened and beside the hinges, the paint had been thumbed away. It had always been here, in the left-hand drawer. He knew every dent and mark upon it. It contained humbugs, striped brown and cream, in cellophane paper. Never any other kind of sweet. The humbugs were brought in by the rich relatives of Miss Reece, on their Sunday afternoon visits. She was not able to eat them herself.

He unwrapped the cellophane and put a humbug inside his mouth, and then he could say nothing, only suck at the tricklings of sweet saliva, and walk about the room, touching things lightly, looking at the picture of 'The Boxing Day Meet*' and the Delights of Britain's Gardens Calendar. Miss Reece lay in the high bed and shook and looked out endlessly on to the dull lawn and the empty avenue. 'She likes me to go and see her,' he had said to Aunt Spencer. The visits were like the words she used to answer his question.

'*Which* room was I born in?'

'Number Six, next to the old nursery, down the corridor from Reece.'

Unchanging, familiar, a comfort. Miss Reece. He had always known her.

'You get along downstairs, your mother's here and waiting.' Wetherby banged the door, and went straight away to Reece, heaving her up the bed, down which she always slipped, little by little every hour, unable to stop herself. He watched for a moment, and remembered the feel of Wetherby's hands, and went quickly away, not looking again into the patient eyes of Miss Reece.

'Now we are going to stay with some people in Lincolnshire, for the weekend. It is nobody you know, and there will not be any children, you would find it so dull. It will be much nicer for you to spend the whole weekend at Aunt Spencer's.'

He ate the crust off a piece of toast, turning it round and round in his mouth. There had been more snow. It squeaked under the soles of his Wellington boots, as they walked to the nursing home. He was carrying his own case.

Aunt Spencer's private sitting-room smelled slightly sweet. There was a great deal of furniture, there were cushions of ruched silk and hand-embroidered pictures and firescreens and samplers and tray-cloths.

'I've cleared a space for you at my desk, you can do your drawing and painting on that,' she said. 'It will keep you out of everybody's way.'

And so he sat for a long time in the stuffy room, fiddling with a penknife and a new box of crayons, trying to draw horses, bored. He found Lincolnshire on a tray-cloth map of Britain, and wondered about his mother and father, trying to picture the house in which they were staying.

'What are the people called?'

'Now I have already told you, darling, you have never met them, they haven't been here, to this house.'

'I want to know their names. I like names.'

She gave him a curious look. 'How funny you are! Well, they are called Pountenay. Mr and Mrs Roger Pountenay. There!'

'Do they play bridge?'

'Oh dear, *I* don't know. Yes, I expect they do.'

'Why don't they have any children in their house?'

'That is not the sort of question you should *ever* ask.'

He did not know whether he would have wanted to go to the house in Lincolnshire, or not. On the wall, beside Aunt Spencer's small desk, was a carved crucifix, and a picture, in soft, blurred colours, of Jesus the Lamb of God.

He began to draw horses again.

When he heard the sound of the door opening, he woke up at once, sitting up in the bed. It was quite dark. A long way downstairs, in the kitchen, Night Nurse, with the lamp and the banked-up fire and the silent row of bells above the swing door. Nobody else. The floorboards creaked on the landing outside. Wetherby. He thought, I could do anything, shout or scream or anything, and nobody would ever hear me, and I cannot run away. He waited for the turning of the knob on his attic bedroom door. Nothing. Sounds, but going a different way, along the corridor and down the stairs.

He got out of bed and put his hands out in front of him, feeling for the door.

All the way down to the basement, the night lamps burned dimly on every landing, at the head of each flight of stairs. When he looked over the banister, he saw the back of Wetherby's head, saw her turn and go out of sight, down the corridor leading to Number Seven, the room of Miss Reece. For no reason, he felt afraid.

There was an ache in his bladder, but he dared not go down to the lavatory, on the first floor, not now. He went back into the attic and groped his way to the bed and lay, squeezing himself tightly between his legs, for fear of wetting the mattress. He did not go to sleep again. Wetherby came back. He waited, and wept with relief when her footsteps went on, past his door. It was all right, it was all right, nothing was going to happen to him. He thought about Reece.

When he woke again, he was still afraid, because he had dreamed and could not remember what he had dreamed, only felt certain that something was wrong. His pyjamas were damp, and there was a cold patch in the sheet. It was dark. There was no sound on the landing, or from downstairs. The night lights were still lit. He felt awake and not awake.

The door of Number Seven was closed. At first he did nothing, he stood outside shivering and feeling the wetness of his pyjamas. Last night, he had seen Miss Reece, he had stayed with her and eaten two sweets and talked about his mother and father in Lincolnshire and how he could not draw horses. 'Turn out her light,' Wetherby said, 'I don't want to go traipsing back up there again.' But he had not done so, it had seemed too early, too unkind, leaving Miss Reece in the dark.

Every morning, after breakfast, every afternoon, and every evening, Wetherby, and somebody helping her, stripped the bedclothes off and lifted up the shaking Miss Reece and placed her on the wooden commode. But yesterday, Wetherby had had to change everything, she said to Huggitt, sheets, blankets, the lot, it went straight through, she was filthy, she didn't try, didn't care, she couldn't bother to lift her finger and press the electric bell. She was getting worse. 'Filthy,' Wetherby said.

He thought, now, that by seeing Miss Reece, he might find comfort for himself.

The room was in darkness. He could hear nothing, until the door closed, and then the faint hissing of the gas.

He thought that she would be dead, and he had never seen a dead person, only the coffins being carried down the stairs by the overcoated men. But Miss Reece lay, propped on the two, full pillows, and he saw that she was not dead, she was breathing deeply, her face a little flushed and pink, in the light of the lamp.

After he had opened the window, he ran, holding his breath, and in the lavatory, on the next landing, was sick. He could not imagine what he might do, could not think of the words he could use to tell them, and be believed. Miss Reece was not dead. He must go back to bed, that was all.

On Saturdays, Wetherby did the early morning teas, and then went away, wearing a green woollen coat and hat, caught a bus to visit her married sister in the country, eleven miles away. She did not come back until very late at night. Tomorrow was Saturday. Nothing could happen to him.

As he closed his door, he heard Wetherby open hers. Downstairs, the clock struck six-thirty. At seven, the rattle of teacups would begin. He did not sleep again.

'Something's wrong with Reece,' Aunt Spencer said. He looked up quickly, from the moist centre of his boiled egg, and saw that Wetherby had come into the kitchen and was watching him, her eyes narrowed and angry, beneath the fleshy lids. He thought, she is dead after all, she is dead and it is my fault because I said nothing. Wetherby has killed her with the gas from the fire. He thought that he had done the right thing, because his father had taught him about gas, and about fires too, and fainting and deep cuts; he said, a boy should not flinch, he should learn to be prepared for any kind of accident from an early age.

'I took her tea up,' Wetherby said. 'She was right enough then.' Her eyes were still on his face.

'Her breathing's bad.' Aunt Spencer opened the enormous bottle of Dettol* and began to pour.

So she was not dead, it was all right. He thought about how he could avoid having to sleep tonight in the attic room, how he might pretend to be ill, so that Aunt Spencer would let him stay on the couch in her own room. Tomorrow, his father and mother would come back from Lincolnshire, nothing would happen, nobody should know.

Aunt Spencer put a mug of hot milk down on the desk. He was trying again to draw horses. Wetherby had gone out, he had seen the movement of her green coat, past the window, and turned his head away. She knows, he thought, she watches me and knows.

'Your *bed* . . .' said Aunt Spencer.

He was silent, remembering the wet patch of mattress.

'You needn't look like that, I shan't tell your mother.'

'Oh.'

When she reached the door, he said, 'I want to go and see Miss Reece.'

'Not now you can't, Doctor Mackay's coming to her any minute.'

'What's the matter?'

'Nothing much, bit of a cold, I shouldn't wonder.' She went out. He remembered her saying, 'Her breathing's bad,' to Wetherby, and he thought of the gas and the window he had opened, on to Miss Reece's head and chest. Outside, there was more snow. He could tell nobody, there was nothing he could say. He wondered how much of it had been his dream.

'If you wrap yourself up sensibly, you can go out and play,' Aunt Spencer said.

He was rolling the head of a snowman round and round the front lawn, enlarging it, when the navy-blue car of Doctor Mackay drew up, outside the nursing home. He thought, now it is all right, now Miss Reece will not die.

The snow had soaked through to his hands, matting the red woollen gloves, and making his flesh burn with cold, as though the fingers had been trapped in a door. He went on with the rolling of the snowman. A little while before lunch, Doctor Mackay came down the steps and got into his navy-blue car and drove carefully away.

In the kitchen, that afternoon, Huggitt and Nurse O'Keefe played Beggar My Neighbour* with him for over an hour, banking up the fire with logs and great chunks of coal. He won four times.

'Have a cherry cough drop,' said Huggitt, sorting her cards, and the smell of them came up, sweet and sharp, into his nostrils. It was snowing again, beyond the window. He thought, this is the best place to be. And perhaps Wetherby's bus will not be able to get back.

At half-past four, Aunt Spencer and O'Keefe went up with the tea trays, and at twenty minutes to five, O'Keefe came down again to the kitchen.

'Reece is dead.'

He had forgotten to pretend that he was ill, and now it was too late for that. He sat on the hearth stool, drinking the hot milk.

'There's a chamber pot under your bed this time,' Aunt Spencer said. He looked away from her, and tried not to think about the dead body of Miss Reece, still for ever, in the high bed. The implications of there being someone else in Number Seven, of the words 'Down the corridor from Reece' ceasing to mean what they had always meant, were too much for him.

'I've telephoned to that sister of hers. Not that they care. They'll be glad to save the money, I daresay . . . mean as they're rich . . . poor soul.' But there seemed to be no alarm, no surprise among them.

At ten past seven, the kitchen door opened and there was Wetherby, shaking the snow from off the shoulders of her bottle-green coat.

'Reece is dead,' said O'Keefe at once.

He looked down into his milk. Wetherby went out into the hallway, in search of Aunt Spencer. Because of the bad weather, she had been shopping, just into the town, she had not tried to go as far as her married sister's.

The fire exploded and spat little slivers of coal out at him, like shell-shot. The flames were blue-green.

'Pneumonia,' he heard Aunt Spencer say, swinging the kitchen door. 'And Mackay's talking nonsense about the Coroner.'

He felt Wetherby come across the room towards him.

'I'll take this one upstairs,' she said, 'and that'll be one job out of the way.'

He saw her feet, misshapen and bumpy with corns, inside

the black nurse's shoes. Beyond them, Aunt Spencer shook a thermometer.

'Yes,' she said, 'and there's a chamber pot for him, under the bed.'

He followed Nurse Wetherby out of the kitchen, and up the first flight of linoleum-covered stairs.

NOTES

Fair Isle (jumper)   (p53)
> a piece of knitwear in a characteristic multi-coloured design, named after *Fair Isle* in the Shetland Islands (off the north coast of Scotland), where the design originated

Sheraton (dressing-table)   (p55)
> a delicate and graceful style of furniture introduced in England in the 1790s (from Thomas Sheraton, an English furniture-maker)

Parkinson's (disease)   (p55)
> a disease of the nervous system that gets worse with time and causes the muscles to become weak and the limbs to shake

needlepoint   (p57)
> embroidery on canvas using small stitches (also called *petit point*)

The Boxing Day Meet   (p58)
> a picture of 'the Hunt' (huntsmen, horses, and hounds) on the day after Christmas Day, a traditional day for hunting

Dettol   (p62)
> the trade name of a liquid disinfectant

Beggar My Neighbour   (p63)
> a card game in which a player tries to capture an opponent's cards

DISCUSSION

1   The story ends on a rather threatening note as Wetherby takes the boy upstairs to put him to bed. Do you think she will say anything to the boy about Miss Reece's death? If so, what? If not, why not? And what else might she do or say?

2   We never learn the boy's name in this story, and we see everything through his eyes. What effect does this have? Would you have liked another viewpoint from time to time, to know what other characters were thinking? How might this have changed the effect of the story?

3   The boy's mother worried, 'vaguely, from time to time,' about whether visiting Miss Reece so often did any harm to the boy. What is your opinion on that? Should young children be kept away from the sick and the dying in case it upsets them?

4   Miss Reece's rich relatives visit her once a week, by turns, 'doing their duty, eating tea and being bored'. Do you think the author is being critical here, implying that the relatives are neglectful and uncaring, and

should do more for Miss Reece? If so, do you agree with this criticism? What else can, or should, people do for a very sick relative like this?

LANGUAGE FOCUS

1 Find these expressions in the story and explain their meaning.
   you won't get under everyone's feet   (p48)
   Why can't I stay at home and be sat with?   (p51)
   I'll come and see to you as well   (p52)
   rolling in money   (p55)
   she isn't soft in the head . . . she's all there   (p56)
   If you wrap yourself up sensibly . . .   (p63)

2 When the boy talks to his mother about Wetherby, he tries to convey his fear of her by describing her unattractive physical attributes:
   'She's ugly . . . Her teeth are all yellow.'

   This earns him a reprimand and fails to communicate his message. What could he have said, which might have made his mother listen to him?

3 The following words are used to describe Nurse Wetherby's actions:
   jabbed, dumping, banged, clashing, shovelling, heaving

   What effect do these words have? What do they suggest about Wetherby's character? Find some more words and phrases in the text that help to show us what Wetherby was like.

ACTIVITIES

1 What actually happened that night, as the boy and Wetherby went to and from Miss Reece's room? Imagine you were a fly on the wall, and write a report describing clearly who must have done what.

2 At the end of the story Aunt Spencer reports that Dr Mackay is 'talking nonsense about the Coroner'. Presumably Dr Mackay sees no medical reason why Miss Reece should suddenly have died of pneumonia, and wishes her death to be investigated. Write a note from him to the Coroner, explaining why you think there should be an inquest.

3 Imagine that the boy tells his mother what he believes Nurse Wetherby has done, but his mother, in her usual dismissive way, does not believe him. Write their conversation.

THE ROCKING-HORSE WINNER

THE AUTHOR

David Herbert Lawrence was born into a coal-miner's family at Eastwood, Nottinghamshire, in 1885, the fourth of five children. Educated at Nottingham University College, he worked as a teacher until forced to give up by ill health. In 1912 he eloped with Frieda Weekley, the wife of his old professor at Nottingham, and they married two years later. His most famous novels are *The White Peacock, Sons and Lovers, The Rainbow, Women in Love*, and *Lady Chatterley's Lover*. Lawrence wrote with great passion and intensity of feeling about people and nature, but his frankness about sex caused some of his books to be suppressed or banned for some years after publication.

Lawrence also wrote poetry, short stories, essays, plays and travel books. He died in France in 1930.

THE STORY

Some stories, such as fairy stories, are not tied to any fixed point in time or place. They often begin with 'There was once a beautiful princess (or a poor fisherman, or a little servant-girl)', and then move straight into a world where the inexplicable can occur without warning at any moment. But whether it is a frog turning into a prince, a goose laying golden eggs, or a boy fighting fearsome giants, there is nearly always a moral underlying the story.

Paul has a mother, a father, two sisters, an uncle. He does not go hungry, he has toys to play with, he lives in a house with servants. But he also has to live with his mother's discontent, which weighs heavily on him. His mother feels she is unlucky, and Paul becomes anxious, desperately anxious, to get to the place where luck is . . .

THE ROCKING-HORSE WINNER

There was a woman who was beautiful, who started with all the advantages, yet she had no luck. She married for love, and the love turned to dust. She had bonny children, yet she felt they had been thrust upon her, and she could not love them. They looked at her coldly, as if they were finding fault with her. And hurriedly she felt she must cover up some fault in herself. Yet what it was that she must cover up she never knew. Nevertheless, when her children were present, she always felt the centre of her heart go hard. This troubled her, and in her manner she was all the more gentle and anxious for her children, as if she loved them very much. Only she herself knew that at the centre of her heart was a hard little place that could not feel love, no, not for anybody. Everybody else said of her: 'She is such a good mother. She adores her children.' Only she herself, and her children themselves, knew it was not so. They read it in each other's eyes.

There were a boy and two little girls. They lived in a pleasant house, with a garden, and they had discreet servants, and felt themselves superior to anyone in the neighbourhood.

Although they lived in style, they felt always an anxiety in the house. There was never enough money. The mother had a small income, and the father had a small income, but not nearly enough for the social position which they had to keep up. The father went into town to some office. But though he had good prospects, these prospects never materialized. There was always the grinding sense of the shortage of money, though the style was always kept up.

At last the mother said: 'I will see if *I* can't make something.' But she did not know where to begin. She racked her brains, and tried this thing and the other, but could not find anything successful. The failure made deep lines come into her face. Her children were growing up, they would have to go to school. There must be more money, there must be more money. The father, who was always very handsome and expensive in his tastes, seemed as if he never *would* be able to do anything worth doing. And the mother, who had a great belief in herself, did not succeed any better, and her tastes were just as expensive.

And so the house came to be haunted by the unspoken phrase: *There must be more money! There must be more money!* The children could hear it all the time, though nobody said it aloud. They heard it at Christmas, when the expensive and splendid toys filled the nursery. Behind the shining modern rocking-horse, behind the smart doll's house, a voice would start whispering: 'There *must* be more money! There *must* be more money!' And the children would stop playing, to listen for a moment. They would look into each other's eyes, to see if they had all heard. And each one saw in the eyes of the other two that they too had heard. 'There *must* be more money! There *must* be more money!'

It came whispering from the springs of the still-swaying rocking-horse, and even the horse, bending his wooden, champing head, heard it. The big doll, sitting so pink and smirking in her new pram, could hear it quite plainly, and seemed to be smirking all the more self-consciously because of it. The foolish puppy, too, that took the place of the teddy-bear, he was looking so extraordinarily foolish for no other reason but that he heard the secret whisper all over the house: 'There *must* be more money!'

Yet nobody ever said it aloud. The whisper was everywhere, and therefore no one spoke it. Just as no one ever says: 'We are breathing!' in spite of the fact that breath is coming and going all the time.

'Mother,' said the boy Paul one day, 'why don't we keep a car of our own? Why do we always use uncle's, or else a taxi?'

'Because we're the poor members of the family,' said the mother.

'But why *are* we, mother?'

'Well – I suppose,' she said slowly and bitterly, 'it's because your father had no luck.'

The boy was silent for some time.

'Is luck money, mother?' he asked, rather timidly.

'No, Paul. Not quite. It's what causes you to have money.'

'Oh!' said Paul vaguely. 'I thought when Uncle Oscar said *filthy lucker*, it meant money.'

'*Filthy lucre* does mean money,' said the mother. 'But it's lucre, not luck.'

'Oh!' said the boy. 'Then what *is* luck, mother?'

'It's what causes you to have money. If you're lucky you have money. That's why it's better to be born lucky than rich. If you're rich, you may lose your money. But if you're lucky, you will always get more money.'

'Oh! Will you? And is father not lucky?'

'Very unlucky, I should say,' she said bitterly.

The boy watched her with unsure eyes.

'Why?' he asked.

'I don't know. Nobody ever knows why one person is lucky and another unlucky.'

'Don't they? Nobody at all? Does *nobody* know?'

'Perhaps God. But He never tells.'

'He ought to, then. And aren't you lucky either, mother?'

'I can't be, if I married an unlucky husband.'

'But by yourself, aren't you?'

'I used to think I was, before I married. Now I think I am very unlucky indeed.'

'Why?'

'Well – never mind! Perhaps I'm not really,' she said.

The child looked at her to see if she meant it. But he saw, by the lines of her mouth, that she was only trying to hide something from him.

'Well, anyhow,' he said stoutly, 'I'm a lucky person.'

'Why?' said his mother, with a sudden laugh.

He stared at her. He didn't even know why he had said it.

'God told me,' he asserted, brazening it out.

'I hope He did, dear!' she said, again with a laugh, but rather bitter.

'He did, mother!'

'Excellent!' said the mother, using one of her husband's exclamations.

The boy saw she did not believe him; or rather, that she paid no attention to his assertion. This angered him somewhere, and made him want to compel her attention.

He went off by himself, vaguely, in a childish way, seeking for the clue to 'luck'. Absorbed, taking no heed of other people, he went about with a sort of stealth, seeking inwardly for luck. He wanted luck, he wanted it, he wanted it. When the two girls were playing dolls in the nursery, he would sit on his big rocking-horse, charging madly into space, with a frenzy that made the little girls peer at him uneasily. Wildly the horse careered, the waving dark hair of the boy tossed, his eyes had a strange glare in them. The little girls dared not speak to him.

When he had ridden to the end of his mad little journey, he climbed down and stood in front of his rocking-horse, staring fixedly into its lowered face. Its red mouth was slightly open, its big eye was wide and glassy-bright.

'Now!' he would silently command the snorting steed. 'Now, take me to where there is luck! Now take me!'

And he would slash the horse on the neck with the little whip he had asked Uncle Oscar for. He *knew* the horse could take him to where there was luck, if only he forced it. So he would mount again and start on his furious ride, hoping at last to get there. He knew he could get there.

'You'll break your horse, Paul!' said the nurse.

'He's always riding like that! I wish he'd leave off!' said his elder sister Joan.

But he only glared down on them in silence. Nurse gave him up. She could make nothing of him. Anyhow, he was growing beyond her.

One day his mother and his Uncle Oscar came in when he was on one of his furious rides. He did not speak to them.

'Hallo, you young jockey! Riding a winner?' said his uncle.

'Aren't you growing too big for a rocking-horse? You're not a very little boy any longer, you know,' said his mother.

But Paul only gave a blue glare from his big, rather close-set eyes. He would speak to nobody when he was in full tilt. His mother watched him with an anxious expression on her face.

At last he suddenly stopped forcing his horse into the mechanical gallop and slid down.

'Well, I got there!' he announced fiercely, his blue eyes still flaring, and his sturdy long legs straddling apart.

'Where did you get to?' asked his mother.

'Where I wanted to go,' he flared back at her.

'That's right, son!' said Uncle Oscar. 'Don't you stop till you get there. What's the horse's name?'

'He doesn't have a name,' said the boy.

'Gets on without all right?' asked the uncle.

'Well, he has different names. He was called Sansovino last week.'

'Sansovino, eh? Won the Ascot*. How did you know this name?'

'He always talks about horse-races with Bassett,' said Joan.

The uncle was delighted to find that his small nephew was posted with all the racing news. Bassett, the young gardener, who had been wounded in the left foot in the war and had got his present job through Oscar Cresswell, whose batman he had been, was a perfect blade of the 'turf'*. He lived in the racing events, and the small boy lived with him.

Oscar Cresswell got it all from Bassett.

'Master Paul comes and asks me, so I can't do more than tell him, sir,' said Bassett, his face terribly serious, as if he were speaking of religious matters.

'And does he ever put anything on a horse he fancies?'

'Well – I don't want to give him away – he's a young sport, a fine sport, sir. Would you mind asking him himself? He sort of takes a pleasure in it, and perhaps he'd feel I was giving him away, sir, if you don't mind.' Bassett was serious as a church.

The uncle went back to his nephew and took him off for a ride in the car.

'Say, Paul, old man, do you ever put anything on a horse?' the uncle asked.

The boy watched the handsome man closely.

'Why, do you think I oughtn't to?' he parried.

'Not a bit of it! I thought perhaps you might give me a tip for the Lincoln*.'

The car sped on into the country, going down to Uncle Oscar's place in Hampshire.

'Honour bright*?' said the nephew.

'Honour bright, son!' said the uncle.

'Well, then, Daffodil.'

'Daffodil! I doubt it, sonny. What about Mirza?'

'I only know the winner,' said the boy. 'That's Daffodil.'

'Daffodil, eh?'

There was a pause. Daffodil was an obscure horse comparatively.

'Uncle!'

'Yes, son?'

'You won't let it go any further, will you? I promised Bassett.'

'Bassett be damned, old man! What's he got to do with it?'

'We're partners. We've been partners from the first. Uncle, he lent me my first five shillings, which I lost. I promised him, honour bright, it was only between me and him; only you gave me that ten-shilling note I started winning with, so I thought you were lucky. You won't let it go any further, will you?'

The boy gazed at his uncle from those big, hot, blue eyes, set rather close together. The uncle stirred and laughed uneasily.

'Right you are, son! I'll keep your tip private. Daffodil, eh? How much are you putting on him?'

'All except twenty pounds,' said the boy. 'I keep that in reserve.'

The uncle thought it a good joke.

'You keep twenty pounds in reserve, do you, you young romancer? What are you betting, then?'

'I'm betting three hundred,' said the boy gravely. 'But it's between you and me, Uncle Oscar! Honour bright?'

The uncle burst into a roar of laughter.

'It's between you and me all right, you young Nat Gould*,' he said, laughing. 'But where's your three hundred?'

'Bassett keeps it for me. We're partners.'

'You are, are you! And what is Bassett putting on Daffodil?'

'He won't go quite as high as I do, I expect. Perhaps he'll go a hundred and fifty.'

'What, pennies?' laughed the uncle.

'Pounds,' said the child, with a surprised look at his uncle. 'Bassett keeps a bigger reserve than I do.'

Between wonder and amusement Uncle Oscar was silent. He pursued the matter no further, but he determined to take his nephew with him to the Lincoln races.

'Now, son,' he said, 'I'm putting twenty on Mirza, and I'll put five on for you on any horse you fancy. What's your pick?'

'Daffodil, uncle.'

'No, not the fiver on Daffodil!'

'I should if it was my own fiver,' said the child.

'Good! Good! Right you are! A fiver for me and a fiver for you on Daffodil.'

The child had never been to a race-meeting before, and his eyes were blue fire. He pursed his mouth tight and watched. A Frenchman just in front had put his money on Lancelot. Wild with excitement, he flayed his arms up and down, yelling '*Lancelot! Lancelot!*' in his French accent.

Daffodil came in first, Lancelot second, Mirza third. The child, flushed and with eyes blazing, was curiously serene. His uncle brought him four five-pound notes, four to one.

'What am I to do with these?' he cried, waving them before the boy's eyes.

'I suppose we'll talk to Bassett,' said the boy. 'I expect I have fifteen hundred now; and twenty in reserve; and this twenty.'

His uncle studied him for some moments.

'Look here, son!' he said. 'You're not serious about Bassett and that fifteen hundred, are you?'

'Yes, I am. But it's between you and me, uncle. Honour bright?'

'Honour bright all right, son! But I must talk to Bassett.'

'If you'd like to be a partner, uncle, with Bassett and me, we could all be partners. Only, you'd have to promise, honour bright, uncle, not to let it go beyond us three. Bassett and I are lucky, and you must be lucky, because it was your ten shillings I started winning with . . .'

Uncle Oscar took both Bassett and Paul into Richmond Park for an afternoon, and there they talked.

'It's like this, you see, sir,' Bassett said. 'Master Paul would get me talking about racing events, spinning yarns, you know, sir. And he was always keen on knowing if I'd made or if I'd lost. It's about a year since, now, that I put five shillings on Blush of Dawn for him: and we lost. Then the luck turned, with that ten shillings he had from you: that we put on Singhalese. And since that time, it's been pretty steady, all things considering. What do you say, Master Paul?'

'We're all right when we're sure,' said Paul. 'It's when we're not quite sure that we go down.'

'Oh, but we're careful then,' said Bassett.

'But when are you *sure*?' smiled Uncle Oscar.

'It's Master Paul, sir,' said Bassett in a secret, religious voice. 'It's as if he had it from heaven. Like Daffodil now, for the Lincoln. That was as sure as eggs.'

'Did you put anything on Daffodil?' asked Oscar Cresswell.

'Yes, sir. I made my bit.'

'And my nephew?'

Bassett was obstinately silent, looking at Paul.

'I made twelve hundred, didn't I, Bassett? I told uncle I was putting three hundred on Daffodil.'

'That's right,' said Bassett, nodding.

'But where's the money?' asked the uncle.

'I keep it safe locked up, sir. Master Paul he can have it any minute he likes to ask for it.'

'What, fifteen hundred pounds?'

'And twenty! And *forty*, that is, with the twenty he made on the course.'

'It's amazing!' said the uncle.

'If Master Paul offers you to be partners, sir, I would, if I were you: if you'll excuse me,' said Bassett.

Oscar Cresswell thought about it.

'I'll see the money,' he said.

They drove home again, and, sure enough, Bassett came round to the garden-house with fifteen hundred pounds in notes. The twenty pounds reserve was left with Joe Glee, in the Turf Commission* deposit.

'You see, it's all right, uncle, when I'm *sure*! Then we go strong, for all we're worth. Don't we, Bassett?'

'We do that, Master Paul.'

'And when are you sure?' said the uncle, laughing.

'Oh, well, sometimes I'm *absolutely* sure, like about Daffodil,' said the boy; 'and sometimes I have an idea; and sometimes I haven't even an idea, have I, Bassett? Then we're careful, because we mostly go down.'

'You do, do you! And when you're sure, like about Daffodil, what makes you sure, sonny?'

'Oh, well, I don't know,' said the boy uneasily. 'I'm sure, you know, uncle; that's all.'

'It's as if he had it from heaven, sir,' Bassett reiterated.

'I should say so!' said the uncle.

But he became a partner. And when the Leger* was coming on Paul was 'sure' about Lively Spark, which was a quite inconsiderable horse. The boy insisted on putting a thousand on the horse, Bassett went for five hundred, and Oscar Cresswell two hundred. Lively Spark came in first, and the betting had been ten to one against him. Paul had made ten thousand.

'You see,' he said, 'I was absolutely sure of him.'

Even Oscar Cresswell had cleared two thousand.

'Look here, son,' he said, 'this sort of thing makes me nervous.'

'It needn't, uncle! Perhaps I shan't be sure again for a long time.'

'But what are you going to do with your money?' asked the uncle.

'Of course,' said the boy, 'I started it for mother. She said she had no luck, because father is unlucky, so I thought if *I* was lucky, it might stop whispering.'

'What might stop whispering?'

'Our house. I *hate* our house for whispering.'

'What does it whisper?'

'Why – why' – the boy fidgeted – 'why, I don't know. But it's always short of money, you know, uncle.'

'I know it, son, I know it.'

'You know people send mother writs, don't you, uncle?'

'I'm afraid I do,' said the uncle.

'And then the house whispers, like people laughing at you behind your back. It's awful, that is! I thought if I was lucky—'

'You might stop it,' added the uncle.

The boy watched him with big blue eyes, that had an uncanny cold fire in them, and he said never a word.

'Well, then!' said the uncle. 'What are we doing?'

'I shouldn't like mother to know I was lucky,' said the boy.

'Why not, son?'

'She'd stop me.'

'I don't think she would.'

'Oh!' – and the boy writhed in an odd way – 'I *don't* want her to know, uncle.'

'All right, son! We'll manage it without her knowing.'

They managed it very easily. Paul, at the other's suggestion, handed over five thousand pounds to his uncle, who deposited it with the family lawyer, who was then to inform Paul's mother that a relative had put five thousand pounds into his hands, which sum was to be paid out a thousand pounds at a time, on the mother's birthday, for the next five years.

'So she'll have a birthday present of a thousand pounds for five successive years,' said Uncle Oscar. 'I hope it won't make it all the harder for her later.'

Paul's mother had her birthday in November. The house had been 'whispering' worse than ever lately, and, even in spite of his luck, Paul could not bear up against it. He was very anxious to see the effect of the birthday letter, telling his mother about the thousand pounds.

When there were no visitors, Paul now took his meals with his parents, as he was beyond the nursery control. His mother went into town nearly every day. She had discovered that she had an odd knack of sketching furs and dress materials, so she worked secretly in the studio of a friend who was the chief 'artist' for the leading drapers. She drew the figures of ladies in furs and ladies in silk and sequins for the newspaper advertisements. This young woman artist earned several thousand pounds a year, but Paul's mother only made several hundreds, and she was again dissatisfied. She so wanted to be first in something, and she did not succeed, even in making sketches for drapery advertisements.

She was down to breakfast on the morning of her birthday. Paul watched her face as she read her letters. He knew the lawyer's letter. As his mother read it, her face hardened and became more expressionless. Then a cold, determined look came on her mouth. She hid the letter under the pile of others, and said not a word about it.

'Didn't you have anything nice in the post for your birthday, mother?' said Paul.

'Quite moderately nice,' she said, her voice cold and absent.

She went away to town without saying more.

But in the afternoon Uncle Oscar appeared. He said Paul's mother had had a long interview with the lawyer, asking if the whole five thousand could not be advanced at once, as she was in debt.

'What do you think, uncle?' said the boy.

'I leave it to you, son.'

'Oh, let her have it, then! We can get some more with the other,' said the boy.

'A bird in the hand is worth two in the bush, laddie!' said Uncle Oscar.

'But I'm sure to *know* for the Grand National*; or the Lincolnshire; or else the Derby*. I'm sure to know for *one* of them,' said Paul.

So Uncle Oscar signed the agreement, and Paul's mother touched the whole five thousand. Then something very curious happened. The voices in the house suddenly went mad, like a chorus of frogs on a spring evening. There were certain new furnishings, and Paul had a tutor. He was *really* going to Eton*, his father's school, in the following autumn. There were flowers in the winter, and a blossoming of the luxury Paul's mother had been used to. And yet the voices in the house, behind the sprays of mimosa and almond-blossom, and from under the piles of iridescent cushions, simply trilled and screamed in a sort of ecstasy: 'There *must* be more money! Oh-h-h; there *must* be more money. Oh, now, now-w! Now-w-w – there *must* be more money! – more than ever! More than ever!'

It frightened Paul terribly. He studied away at his Latin and Greek with his tutor. But his intense hours were spent with Bassett. The Grand National had gone by; he had not ' known', and had lost a hundred pounds. Summer was at hand. He was in agony for the Lincoln. But even for the Lincoln he didn't 'know', and he lost fifty pounds. He became wild-eyed and strange, as if something were going to explode in him.

'Let it alone, son! Don't you bother about it!' urged Uncle Oscar. But it was as if the boy couldn't really hear what his uncle was saying.

'I've got to know for the Derby! I've got to know for the Derby!' the child reiterated, his big blue eyes blazing with a sort of madness.

His mother noticed how overwrought he was.

'You'd better go to the seaside. Wouldn't you like to go now to the seaside, instead of waiting? I think you'd better,' she said, looking down at him anxiously, her heart curiously heavy because of him.

But the child lifted his uncanny blue eyes.

'I couldn't possibly go before the Derby, mother!' he said. 'I couldn't possibly!'

'Why not?' she said, her voice becoming heavy when she was opposed. 'Why not? You can still go from the seaside to see the

Derby with your Uncle Oscar, if that's what you wish. No need for you to wait here. Besides, I think you care too much about these races. It's a bad sign. My family has been a gambling family, and you won't know till you grow up how much damage it has done. But it has done damage. I shall have to send Bassett away, and ask Uncle Oscar not to talk racing to you, unless you promise to be reasonable about it: go away to the seaside and forget it. You're all nerves!'

'I'll do what you like, mother, so long as you don't send me away till after the Derby,' the boy said.

'Send you away from where? Just from this house?'

'Yes,' he said, gazing at her.

'Why, you curious child, what makes you care about this house so much, suddenly? I never knew you loved it.'

He gazed at her without speaking. He had a secret within a secret, something he had not divulged, even to Bassett or to his Uncle Oscar.

But his mother, after standing undecided and a little bit sullen for some moments, said:

'Very well, then! Don't go to the seaside till after the Derby, if you don't wish it. But promise me you won't let your nerves go to pieces. Promise you won't think so much about horse-racing, and *events*, as you call them!'

'Oh no,' said the boy casually. 'I won't think much about them, mother. You needn't worry. I wouldn't worry, mother, if I were you.'

'If you were me and I were you,' said his mother, 'I wonder what we *should* do!'

'But you know you needn't worry, mother, don't you?' the boy repeated.

'I should be awfully glad to know it,' she said wearily.

'Oh, well, you *can*, you know. I mean, you *ought* to know you needn't worry,' he insisted.

'Ought I? Then I'll see about it,' she said.

Paul's secret of secrets was his wooden horse, that which had no name. Since he was emancipated from a nurse and a nursery-governess, he had had his rocking-horse removed to his own bedroom at the top of the house.

'Surely you're too big for a rocking-horse!' his mother had remonstrated.

'Well, you see, mother, till I can have a *real* horse, I like to have *some* sort of animal about,' had been his quaint answer.

'Do you feel he keeps you company?' she laughed.

'Oh yes! He's very good, he always keeps me company, when I'm there,' said Paul.

So the horse, rather shabby, stood in an arrested prance in the boy's bedroom.

The Derby was drawing near, and the boy grew more and more tense. He hardly heard what was spoken to him, he was very frail, and his eyes were really uncanny. His mother had sudden strange seizures of uneasiness about him. Sometimes, for half an hour, she would feel a sudden anxiety about him that was almost anguish. She wanted to rush to him at once, and know he was safe.

Two nights before the Derby, she was at a big party in town, when one of her rushes of anxiety about her boy, her first-born, gripped her heart till she could hardly speak. She fought with the feeling, might and main*, for she believed in common sense. But it was too strong. She had to leave the dance and go downstairs to telephone to the country. The children's nursery-governess was terribly surprised and startled at being rung up in the night.

'Are the children all right, Miss Wilmot?'

'Oh yes, they are quite all right.'

'Master Paul? Is he all right?'

'He went to bed as right as a trivet*. Shall I run up and look at him?'

'No,' said Paul's mother reluctantly. 'No! Don't trouble. It's all right. Don't sit up. We shall be home fairly soon.' She did not want her son's privacy intruded upon.

'Very good,' said the governess.

It was about one o'clock when Paul's mother and father drove up to their house. All was still. Paul's mother went to her room and slipped off her white fur cloak. She had told her maid not to wait up for her. She heard her husband downstairs, mixing a whisky and soda.

And then, because of the strange anxiety at her heart, she stole upstairs to her son's room. Noiselessly she went along the upper corridor. Was there a faint noise? What was it?

She stood, with arrested muscles, outside his door, listening. There was a strange, heavy, and yet not loud noise. Her heart stood still. It was a soundless noise, yet rushing and powerful. Something huge, in violent, hushed motion. What was it? What in God's name was it? She ought to know. She felt that she knew the noise. She knew what it was.

Yet she could not place it. She couldn't say what it was. And on and on it went, like a madness.

Softly, frozen with anxiety and fear, she turned the door-handle.

The room was dark. Yet in the space near the window, she heard and saw something plunging to and fro. She gazed in fear and amazement.

Then suddenly she switched on the light, and saw her son, in his green pyjamas, madly surging on the rocking-horse. The blaze of light suddenly lit him up, as he urged the wooden horse, and lit her up, as she stood, blonde, in her dress of pale green and crystal, in the doorway.

'Paul!' she cried. 'Whatever are you doing?'

'It's Malabar!' he screamed in a powerful, strange voice. 'It's Malabar!'

His eyes blazed at her for one strange and senseless second, as he ceased urging his wooden horse. Then he fell with a crash to the ground, and she, all her tormented motherhood flooding upon her, rushed to gather him up.

But he was unconscious, and unconscious he remained, with some brain-fever. He talked and tossed, and his mother sat stonily by his side.

'Malabar! It's Malabar! Bassett, Bassett, I *know*! It's Malabar!'

So the child cried, trying to get up and urge the rocking-horse that gave him his inspiration.

'What does he mean by Malabar?' asked the heart-frozen mother.

'I don't know,' said the father stonily.

'What does he mean by Malabar?' she asked her brother Oscar.

'It's one of the horses running for the Derby,' was the answer.

And, in spite of himself, Oscar Cresswell spoke to Bassett, and himself put a thousand on Malabar: at fourteen to one.

The third day of the illness was critical: they were waiting for a change. The boy, with his rather long, curly hair, was tossing ceaselessly on the pillow. He neither slept nor regained consciousness, and his eyes were like blue stones. His mother sat, feeling her heart had gone, turned actually into a stone.

In the evening, Oscar Cresswell did not come, but Bassett sent a message, saying could he come up for one moment, just one moment? Paul's mother was very angry at the intrusion, but on second thoughts she agreed. The boy was the same. Perhaps Bassett might bring him to consciousness.

The gardener, a shortish fellow with a little brown moustache and sharp little brown eyes, tiptoed into the room, touched his imaginary cap to Paul's mother, and stole to the bedside, staring with glittering, smallish eyes at the tossing, dying child.

'Master Paul!' he whispered. 'Master Paul! Malabar came in first all right, a clean win. I did as you told me. You've made over seventy thousand pounds, you have; you've got over eighty thousand. Malabar came in all right, Master Paul.'

'Malabar! Malabar! Did I say Malabar, mother? Did I say Malabar? Do you think I'm lucky, mother? I knew Malabar, didn't I? Over eighty thousand pounds! I call that lucky, don't you, mother? Over eighty thousand pounds! I knew, didn't I know I knew? Malabar came in all right. If I ride my horse till I'm sure, then I tell you, Bassett, you can go as high as you like. Did you go for all you were worth, Bassett?'

'I went a thousand on it, Master Paul.'

'I never told you, mother, that if I can ride my horse, and *get there*, then I'm absolutely sure – oh, absolutely! Mother, did I ever tell you? I *am* lucky!'

'No, you never did,' said his mother.

But the boy died in the night.

And even as he lay dead, his mother heard her brother's voice saying to her: 'My God, Hester, you're eighty-odd thousand to the good, and a poor devil of a son to the bad. But, poor devil, poor devil, he's best gone out of a life where he rides his rocking-horse to find a winner.'

NOTES

Ascot, Lincoln, Derby (pp 74, 75, 81)

  racecourses near these towns, where there are famous horse races every
  year

blade (of the 'turf') (p75)

  (old-fashioned) a lively, spirited, stylish young man (the 'turf' is a
  general term for the sport of horse-racing)

honour bright (p75)

  (colloquial, old-fashioned) an exclamation promising very seriously that
  you will do something or that something is true; also used as a question

Nat Gould (p76)

  a name signifying someone very knowledgeable about horse-racing (Nat
  Gould was an author of sporting novels and reminiscences)

Turf Commission (p78)

  Lawrence probably meant turf commissioner or accountant, i.e. a
  bookmaker (someone who deals in betting on horse races)

the Leger, the Grand National (pp 79, 81)

  names of famous horse races (at Doncaster and Liverpool respectively)

Eton (p82)

  a public (i.e. fee-paying) school; one of the most well-known – and
  expensive – in Britain

might and main (p84)

  (literary) with all one's strength or power

trivet (as right as a trivet) (p84)

  (idiom, old-fashioned) perfectly all right

DISCUSSION

1 What do you think the moral of this story is? Is it a relevant one for
   the modern world?

2 In most fairy stories there is usually a villain, or villains, of some kind
   – characters who represent the unpleasant, cruel, or evil sides of human
   nature. Who do you see as the 'villain' in this story? Is it the mother,
   whose insatiable desire for wealth and possessions leads to her son's
   destruction? Or are Bassett and Uncle Oscar equally responsible for
   Paul's sufferings?

3 Did you find the ending of the story surprising? Fairy stories often have
   happy endings (. . . 'and they lived happily ever after'). Would you have

preferred a happy ending to this story? Why? Would it have made the story more effective, or less?

LANGUAGE FOCUS

1 Find these expressions in the story and explain what they mean.
   the style was always kept up   (p70)
   I wish he'd leave off   (p74)
   She could make nothing of him   (p74)
   I don't want to give him away   (p75)
   do you ever put anything on a horse?   (p75)
   You won't let it go any further, will you?   (p76)
   it's between you and me   (p76)
   Paul could not bear up against it   (p80)
   A bird in the hand is worth two in the bush   (p81)
   promise me you won't let your nerves go to pieces   (p83)
   all her tormented motherhood flooding upon her   (p86)
   you're eighty-odd thousand to the good   (p87)

ACTIVITIES

1 Do you think *The Rocking-Horse Winner* is a good title for this story? Think of some titles to reflect different aspects of the story: for example, the supernatural elements, the horse-racing, the betting, Paul's obsession, his relationship with his mother, the sad ending.

2 If this story had a happy ending, where would be the best place to change direction? Would it be at the point where Bassett brings the news to Paul about Malabar winning the Derby? Or earlier, for example, when Paul's mother notices how overwrought he is and tries to persuade him to go to the seaside? Choose the moment you prefer, and write a new ending for the story – one which you would call a 'happy' ending. Use some of these ideas or think of your own.
   • Paul recovers from his fever and never bets again.
   • The mother realizes her children are more important than wealth.
   • Paul recovers, and his mother joins the betting partnership.
   • Paul's mother dies, and the house stops whispering about money.
   • Uncle Oscar learns Paul's secret and burns the rocking-horse.
   • Paul becomes a normal boy but still enjoys going to the races.

THE OPEN WINDOW

THE AUTHOR

Hector Hugh Munro, the British novelist and short-story writer known as Saki, was born in Burma in 1870 and brought up in England. He travelled widely and became a successful journalist; for six years he acted as correspondent for *The Morning Post* in Poland, Russia, and Paris. He is best known for his short stories, which are humorous, sometimes with a touch of black humour, and full of biting wit and bizarre situations. Some of his short-story collections are *Reginald in Russia and Other Sketches*, *The Chronicles of Clovis*, and *Beasts and Superbeasts*. He also published two novels, *The Unbearable Bassington* and *When William Came*. Saki was killed in France during the First World War, in 1916.

THE STORY

Children often have vivid imaginations, and fewer inhibitions than adults about giving the imagination full rein. Perhaps the division between fiction and reality, truth and lies is a tiresome adult preoccupation, best ignored by any young creative artist.

Framton Nuttel is a man with a nervous disposition. He has come to stay in a quiet country village, to rest and relax and take care of his poor nerves. His sister, briskly determined to ensure he has a social life, has given him letters of introduction to various local people, whom she had met a few years previously. Framton dutifully makes a formal visit to a Mrs Sappleton, and is greeted by her niece, a young lady of fifteen, who, while waiting for her aunt to appear, kindly undertakes to explain to the visitor a little of the family's history . . .

The Open Window

'My aunt will be down presently, Mr Nuttel,' said a very self-possessed young lady of fifteen; 'in the meantime you must try and put up with me.'

Framton Nuttel endeavoured to say the correct something which should duly flatter the niece of the moment without unduly discounting the aunt that was to come. Privately he doubted more than ever whether these formal visits on a succession of total strangers would do much towards helping the nerve cure which he was supposed to be undergoing.

'I know how it will be,' his sister had said when he was preparing to migrate to this rural retreat; 'you will bury yourself down there and not speak to a living soul, and your nerves will be worse than ever from moping. I shall just give you letters of introduction to all the people I know there. Some of them, as far as I can remember, were quite nice.'

Framton wondered whether Mrs Sappleton, the lady to whom he was presenting one of the letters of introduction, came into the nice division.

'Do you know many of the people round here?' asked the niece, when she judged that they had had sufficient silent communion.

'Hardly a soul,' said Framton. 'My sister was staying here, at the rectory, you know, some four years ago, and she gave me letters of introduction to some of the people here.'

He made the last statement in a tone of distinct regret.

'Then you know practically nothing about my aunt?' pursued the self-possessed young lady.

'Only her name and address,' admitted the caller. He was wondering whether Mrs Sappleton was in the married or widowed state. An undefinable something about the room seemed to suggest masculine habitation.

'Her great tragedy happened just three years ago,' said the child; 'that would be since your sister's time.'

'Her tragedy?' asked Framton; somehow in this restful country spot tragedies seemed out of place.

'You may wonder why we keep that window wide open on an October afternoon,' said the niece, indicating a large French window* that opened on to a lawn.

'It is quite warm for the time of the year,' said Framton; 'but has that window got anything to do with the tragedy?'

'Out through that window, three years ago to a day, her husband and her two young brothers went off for their day's shooting. They never came back. In crossing the moor to their favourite snipe*-shooting ground they were all three engulfed in a treacherous piece of bog. It had been that dreadful wet summer, you know, and places that were safe in other years gave way suddenly without warning. Their bodies were never recovered. That was the dreadful part of it.' Here the child's voice lost its self-possessed note and became falteringly human. 'Poor aunt always thinks that they will come back some day, they and the little brown spaniel that was lost with them, and walk in at that window just as they used to do. That is why the window is kept open every evening till it is quite dusk. Poor dear aunt, she has often told me how they went out, her husband with his white waterproof coat over his arm, and Ronnie, her youngest brother, singing, "Bertie, why do you bound?" as he always did to tease her, because she said it got on her nerves. Do you know, sometimes on still, quiet evenings like this, I almost get a creepy feeling that they will all walk in through that window—'

She broke off with a little shudder. It was a relief to Framton when the aunt bustled into the room with a whirl of apologies for being late in making her appearance.

'I hope Vera has been amusing you?' she said.

'She has been very interesting,' said Framton.

'I hope you don't mind the open window,' said Mrs Sappleton briskly; 'my husband and brothers will be home directly from shooting, and they always come in this way. They've been out for snipe in the marshes today, so they'll make a fine mess over my poor carpets. So like you men-folk, isn't it?'

She rattled on cheerfully about the shooting and the scarcity of birds, and the prospects for duck in the winter. To Framton it was all purely horrible. He made a desperate but only partially successful effort to turn the talk on to a less ghastly topic; he was conscious that his hostess was giving him only a fragment of her attention, and her eyes were constantly straying past him to the open window and the lawn beyond. It was certainly an unfortunate coincidence that he should have paid his visit on this tragic anniversary.

'The doctors agree in ordering me complete rest, an absence of mental excitement, and avoidance of anything in the nature of violent physical exercise,' announced Framton, who laboured under the tolerably wide-spread delusion that total strangers and chance acquaintances are hungry for the least detail of one's ailments and infirmities, their cause and cure. 'On the matter of diet they are not so much in agreement,' he continued.

'No?' said Mrs Sappleton, in a voice which only replaced a yawn at the last moment. Then she suddenly brightened into alert attention – but not to what Framton was saying.

'Here they are at last!' she cried. 'Just in time for tea, and don't they look as if they were muddy up to the eyes!'

Framton shivered slightly and turned towards the niece with a look intended to convey sympathetic comprehension. The child was staring out through the open window with dazed horror in her eyes. In a chill shock of nameless fear Framton swung round in his seat and looked in the same direction.

In the deepening twilight three figures were walking across the lawn towards the window; they all carried guns under their arms, and one of them was additionally burdened with a white coat hung over his shoulders. A tired brown spaniel kept close at their heels. Noiselessly they neared the house, and then a hoarse young voice chanted out of the dusk: 'I said, Bertie, why do you bound?'

Framton grabbed wildly at his stick and hat; the hall-door, the gravel-drive, and the front gate were dimly noted stages in his headlong retreat. A cyclist coming along the road had to run into the hedge to avoid imminent collision.

'Here we are, my dear,' said the bearer of the white mackintosh, coming in through the window; 'fairly muddy, but most of it's dry. Who was that who bolted out as we came up?'

'A most extraordinary man, a Mr Nuttel,' said Mrs Sappleton; 'could only talk about his illnesses, and dashed off without a word of goodbye or apology when you arrived. One would think he had seen a ghost.'

'I expect it was the spaniel,' said the niece calmly; 'he told me he had a horror of dogs. He was once hunted into a cemetery somewhere on the banks of the Ganges* by a pack of pariah* dogs, and had to spend the night in a newly dug grave with the creatures snarling and grinning and foaming just above him. Enough to make any one lose their nerve.'

Romance at short notice was her speciality.

NOTES

French window   (p93)
   a glass door that leads to a garden or balcony
snipe   (p93)
   a bird that lives on wet ground and that people hunt for sport or food
Ganges   (p95)
   a river in the north of India, sacred to Hindus
pariah dogs (also pye-dog, pie-dog)   (p95)
   homeless dogs of mixed breed, found especially in Asia

DISCUSSION

1   Vera cunningly makes sure that Framton Nuttel will have no reason to
    suspect her story is a fiction. What three pieces of necessary
    information does she extract from Framton before she begins her
    dramatic tale?

2   Do you think that Vera told her story in a plausible way, or did you
    suspect at some point that she was setting up an elaborate joke? If so,
    did that lessen your enjoyment, or is an expected conclusion a satisfying
    way to finish a story?

3   If Framton had stayed in the room when the three men returned, he
    would soon have realized that the men were not ghosts, and that Vera
    had been pulling his leg all along. What do you think he would have
    said or done, and how would Vera have handled the situation? What
    would *you* do or say if someone played a trick like that on you?

LANGUAGE FOCUS

1   When Vera says to Framton Nuttel that 'in the meantime you must try
    and put up with me', Framton has to give a polite response. Think of
    an appropriate way of replying that would 'duly flatter the niece of the
    moment without unduly discounting the aunt that was to come'.

2   For humorous effect, Saki often uses quite ornate language. Find the
    following in the text and rephrase them in a simple, direct style.
    • *. . . when he was preparing to migrate to this rural retreat.*   (p92)
    • *. . . when she judged that they had had sufficient silent
       communion.*   (p92)

- *An indefinable something about the room seemed to suggest masculine habitation.* (p93)
- *. . . he was conscious that his hostess was giving him only a fragment of her attention . . .* (p94)
- *. . . who laboured under the tolerably wide-spread delusion that total strangers and chance acquaintances are hungry for the least detail of one's ailments and infirmities . . .* (p94)
- *. . . the hall-door, the gravel-drive, and the front gate were dimly noted stages in his headlong retreat.* (p95)

ACTIVITIES

1 The story is told from Framton's point of view, but what did Vera think of him, and why did she play such a trick on him? Write a short entry for her diary that day, describing Framton through her eyes and the success of her trick. You could begin like this:

Such a BORING little man came to visit today. Luckily, my aunt was upstairs when he arrived . . .

2 Saki's story was written in an era when everybody wrote letters. Imagine that after Framton's visit to Mrs Sappleton the following short letters were written. Use these notes, or your own ideas, and write all six letters. Keep them very short and to the point.

a) Mrs Sappleton to Framton's sister
your brother's visit / extraordinary behaviour / though perhaps understandable / niece / Ganges / pariah dogs

b) Framton's sister to Framton
what on earth? / Mrs Sappleton's niece / Ganges / pariah dogs / nerves going to pieces / most embarrassing / come home at once

c) Framton to his sister
what? / never been to India / ghastly experience / anniversary of tragedy / open window / three ghosts / with my own eyes

d) Framton's sister to Framton
what tragedy? / husband / brothers / alive and well / who told you? / joke in dreadful taste

e) Framton to Vera
tragedy / pariah dogs / wild inventions / why, why?

f) Vera to Framton
so sorry / thinking of a *different* aunt / pariah dogs story in newspaper / a Mr F. Nuttel / not you?

NEXT TERM, WE'LL MASH YOU

THE AUTHOR

Penelope Lively was born in Egypt in 1933 and spent her childhood there. After World War II she settled in England, and studied history at St Anne's College, Oxford. She began her career as a writer for children, and many of her stories show a preoccupation with the effect of the past on the present, often with a supernatural element. Her best-known children's book is *The Ghost of Thomas Kempe* (1973), which won the Carnegie Medal (a prize for the best children's book of the year). In 1977 she began to write novels and short stories for adults, and has won several literary prizes for them. Titles include *The Road to Lichfield*, *Judgement Day*, *According to Mark*, and *Moon Tiger*, which won the Booker Prize in 1987.

THE STORY

Which of us does not remember our schooldays? They might have been the best or the worst days of our life, but in either case they had a great influence on us, whether for good or ill. As Saki wrote in one of his short stories, with his usual biting humour, 'You can't expect a boy to be vicious till he's been to a good school.'

A new school is being selected for Charles Manders. It will be a boarding school for boys aged 8 to 13, and his parents have almost decided on St Edward's Preparatory School. As they drive into the school on their inspection visit, the parents discuss the fees, admire the school grounds, and hope they will be offered some refreshment. In the back of the car, young Charles, in his shiny new clothes, sits silently, watching and listening . . .

Next Term, We'll Mash You

Inside the car it was quiet, the noise of the engine even and subdued, the air just the right temperature, the windows tight-fitting. The boy sat on the back seat, a box of chocolates, unopened, beside him, and a comic, folded. The trim Sussex landscape flowed past the windows: cows, white-fenced fields, highly-priced period houses. The sunlight was glassy, remote as a coloured photograph. The backs of the two heads in front of him swayed with the motion of the car.

His mother half-turned to speak to him. 'Nearly there now, darling.'

The father glanced downwards at his wife's wrist. 'Are we all right for time?'

'Just right. Nearly twelve.'

'I could do with a drink. Hope they lay something on.'

'I'm sure they will. The Wilcoxes say they're awfully nice people. Not really the schoolmaster-type at all, Sally says.'

The man said, 'He's an Oxford chap*.'

'Is he? You didn't say.'

'Mmn.'

'Of course, the fees are that much higher than the Seaford place.'

'Fifty quid or so. We'll have to see.'

The car turned right, between white gates and high, dark, tight-clipped hedges. The whisper of the road under the tyres changed to the crunch of gravel. The child, staring sideways, read black lettering on a white board: 'St Edward's Preparatory* School. Please Drive Slowly'. He shifted on the seat, and the leather sucked at the bare skin under his knees, stinging.

The mother said, 'It's a lovely place. Those must be the playing-fields. Look, darling, there are some of the boys.' She clicked open her handbag, and the sun caught her mirror and flashed in the child's eyes; the comb went through her hair and he saw the grooves it left, neat as distant ploughing.

'Come on, then, Charles, out you get.'

The building was red brick, early nineteenth century, spreading out long arms in which windows glittered blackly. Flowers, trapped in neat beds, were alternate red and white. They went up the steps, the man, the woman, and the child two paces behind.

The woman, the mother, smoothing down a skirt that would be ridged from sitting, thought: I like the way they've got the maid all done up properly. The little white apron and all that. She's foreign, I suppose. Au pair. Very nice. If he comes here there'll be Speech Days and that kind of thing. Sally Wilcox says it's quite dressy – she got that cream linen coat for coming down here. You can see why it costs a bomb. Great big grounds and only an hour and a half from London.

They went into a room looking out onto a terrace. Beyond, dappled lawns, gently shifting trees, black and white cows grazing behind iron railings. Books, leather chairs, a table with magazines – *Country Life, The Field, The Economist.* 'Please, if you would wait here. The Headmaster won't be long.'

Alone, they sat, inspected. 'I like the atmosphere, don't you, John?'

'Very pleasant, yes.' Four hundred a term, near enough. You can tell it's a cut above the Seaford place, though, or the one at St Albans. Bob Wilcox says quite a few City people* send their boys here. One or two of the merchant bankers, those kind of people. It's the sort of contact that would do no harm at all. You meet someone, get talking at a cricket match or what have you . . . Not at all a bad thing.

'All right, Charles? You didn't get sick in the car, did you?'

The child had black hair, slicked down smooth to his head. His ears, too large, jutted out, transparent in the light from the window, laced with tiny, delicate veins. His clothes had the shine and crease of newness. He looked at the books, the dark brown pictures, his parents, said nothing.

'Come here, let me tidy your hair.'

The door opened. The child hesitated, stood up, sat, then rose again with his father.

'Mr and Mrs Manders? How very nice to meet you – I'm Margaret Spokes, and will you please forgive my husband who is tied up with some wretch who broke the cricket pavilion window and will be just a few more minutes. We try to be organised but a schoolmaster's day is always just that bit unpredictable. Do please sit down and what will you have to revive you after that beastly drive? You live in Finchley*, is that right?'

'Hampstead*, really,' said the mother. 'Sherry would be lovely.' She worked over the headmaster's wife from shoes to hairstyle, pricing and assessing. Shoes old but expensive – Russell and Bromley*. Good skirt. Blouse could be Marks and Sparks* – not sure. Real pearls. Super Victorian ring. She's not gone to any particular trouble – that's just what she'd wear anyway. You can be confident, with a voice like that, of course. Sally Wilcox says she knows all sorts of people.

The headmaster's wife said, 'I don't know how much you know about us. Prospectuses don't tell you a thing, do they? We'll look round everything in a minute, when you've had a chat with my husband. I gather you're friends of the Wilcoxes, by the way. I'm awfully fond of Simon – he's down for Winchester*, of course, but I expect you know that.'

The mother smiled over her sherry. Oh, I know that all right. Sally Wilcox doesn't let you forget that.

'And this is Charles? My dear, we've been forgetting all about you! In a minute I'm going to borrow Charles and take him off to meet some of the boys because after all you're choosing a school for him, aren't you, and not for you, so he ought to know what he might be letting himself in for and it shows we've got nothing to hide.'

The parents laughed. The father, sherry warming his guts, thought that this was an amusing woman. Not attractive, of course, a bit homespun, but impressive all the same. Partly the voice, of course; it takes a bloody expensive education to produce a voice like that. And other things, of course. Background and all that stuff.

'I think I can hear the thud of the Fourth Form coming in from games, which means my husband is on the way, and then I shall leave you with him while I take Charles off to the common-room.'

For a moment the three adults centred on the child, looking, judging. The mother said, 'He looks so hideously pale, compared to those boys we saw outside.'

'My dear, that's London, isn't it? You just have to get them out, to get some colour into them. Ah, here's James. James – Mr and Mrs Manders. You remember, Bob Wilcox was mentioning at Sports Day . . .'

The headmaster reflected his wife's style, like paired cards in Happy Families*. His clothes were mature rather than old, his skin well-scrubbed, his shoes clean, his geniality untainted by the least condescension. He was genuinely sorry to have kept them waiting, but in this business one lurches from one minor crisis to the next . . . And this is Charles? Hello, there, Charles. His large hand rested for a moment on the child's head, quite extinguishing the thin, dark hair. It was as though he had but to clench his fingers to crush the skull. But he took his hand away and moved the parents to the window, to observe the mutilated cricket pavilion, with indulgent laughter.

And the child is borne away by the headmaster's wife. She never touches him or tells him to come, but simply bears him away like some relentless tide, down corridors and through swinging glass doors, towing him like a frail craft, not bothering to look back to see if he is following, confident in the strength of magnetism, or obedience.

And delivers him to a room where boys are scattered among inky tables and rungless chairs and sprawled on a mangy carpet. There is a scampering, and a rising, and a silence falling, as she opens the door.

'Now this is the Lower Third, Charles, who you'd be with if you come to us in September. Boys, this is Charles Manders, and I want you to tell him all about things and answer any questions he wants to ask. You can believe about half of what they say, Charles, and they will tell you the most fearful lies about the food, which is excellent.'

The boys laugh and groan; amiable, exaggerated groans. They must like the headmaster's wife: there is licensed repartee. They look at her with bright eyes in open, eager faces. Someone leaps to hold the door for her, and close it behind her. She is gone.

The child stands in the centre of the room, and it draws in around him. The circle of children contracts, faces are only a yard or so from him; strange faces, looking, assessing.

Asking questions. They help themselves to his name, his age, his school. Over their heads he sees beyond the window an inaccessible world of shivering trees and high racing clouds and his voice which has floated like a feather in the dusty schoolroom air dies altogether and he becomes mute, and he stands in the middle of them with shoulders humped, staring down at feet: grubby plimsolls and kicked brown sandals. There is a noise in his ears like rushing water, a torrential din out of which voices boom, blotting each other out so that he cannot always hear the words. Do you? they say, and Have you? and What's your? and the faces, if he looks up, swing into one another in kaleidoscopic patterns and the floor under his feet is unsteady, lifting and falling.

And out of the noises comes one voice that is complete, that he can hear. 'Next term, we'll mash you,' it says. 'We always mash new boys.'

And a bell goes, somewhere beyond doors and down corridors, and suddenly the children are all gone, clattering away and leaving him there with the heaving floor and the walls that shift and swing, and the headmaster's wife comes back and tows him away, and he is with his parents again, and they are getting into the car, and the high hedges skim past the car windows once more, in the other direction, and the gravel under the tyres changes to black tarmac.

'Well?'

'I liked it, didn't you?' The mother adjusted the car around her, closing windows, shrugging into her seat.

'Very pleasant, really. Nice chap.'

'I liked him. Not quite so sure about her.'

'It's pricey, of course.'

'All the same . . .'

'Money well spent, though. One way and another.'

'Shall we settle it, then?'

'I think so. I'll drop him a line.'

The mother pitched her voice a notch higher to speak to the child in the back of the car. 'Would you like to go there, Charles? Like Simon Wilcox. Did you see that lovely gym, and the swimming-pool? And did the other boys tell you all about it?'

The child does not answer. He looks straight ahead of him, at the road coiling beneath the bonnet of the car. His face is haggard with anticipation.

NOTES

an Oxford chap (p100)
  a chap *(informal)* educated at Oxford university
preparatory school (p100)
  a private (fee-paying) school for children up to the age of 13
City people (p101)
  people who work in the financial institutions of the City of London
Finchley, Hampstead (p102)
  two adjacent districts in London; Hampstead is the more fashionable
  and 'superior' district, so would be the 'better' address
Russell and Bromley (p102)
  the name of a British shop selling expensive, high quality shoes
Marks and Sparks (p102)
  an informal name for Marks and Spencer, a famous British department
  store (but a name with less snob value than Russell and Bromley)
down for Winchester (p102)
  has his name down to go to Winchester School, a very old and famous
  public (fee-paying) school in the south of England
Happy Families (p103)
  a card game in which members of the same 'family' have to be paired,
  e.g. Mr Bun the Baker / Mrs Bun the Baker's wife

DISCUSSION

1 While they are waiting for the headmaster and his wife to appear, what
   do Mr and Mrs Manders think about? And at the end of the story, do
   they make their decision about the school before or after asking Charles
   if he would like to go there? – a question that Charles doesn't answer.
   What does all this tell us about Charles's parents and their relationship
   with their son?

2 What impression do we get of the headmaster and his wife? Did you
   feel they were unpleasant people, likely to be unkind to the boys in their
   charge? Or is their school probably quite a happy place? What clues are
   we given in the story?

3 The story is told from the point of view of Charles's parents. Charles
   himself never speaks, and we are given only a few clues as to his state
   of mind; yet we are painfully aware of it. How has the author achieved
   this? Give examples.

4 Children can be very cruel, and bullying is often a problem in schools. If teachers know that their pupils 'always mash new boys', for example, should they do something about it, or is it better to let the children sort out this kind of thing for themselves? Why, or why not?

LANGUAGE FOCUS

1 Find these phrases and idiomatic expressions in the text, and rephrase them in your own words.

Hope they lay something on. (p100)
. . . it's quite dressy. (p101)
. . . it costs a bomb. (p101)
You can tell it's a cut above the Seaford place . . . (p101)
. . . or what have you. (p101)
. . . who is tied up with some wretch (p102)
. . . she knows all sorts of people (p102)
. . . what he might be letting himself in for (p103)
Background and all that stuff. (p103)
Next term, we'll mash you. (p105)
It's pricey. (p105)
I'll drop him a line. (p105)

2 From the top of page 104 to the end of the third paragraph on page 105, and also in the final paragraph, the past tense narration used elsewhere switches to a present tense narration. Why do you think the author did this, and what effect does it have?

3 The story ends with the striking phrase, 'haggard with anticipation'. Is there anything unexpected about this phrase? What other words could be used in place of 'anticipation'? Do they have the same effect?

ACTIVITIES

1 Imagine that poor Charles is a more assertive kind of boy, and on the way home in the car makes it clear how he feels about the new school. Write the dialogue between him and his parents. Who do you think would win the argument?

2 What do you think the other boys thought of Charles? Write a diary entry for one of the boys in the common-room, describing the entry of Mrs Stokes with Charles, and the interrogation that followed.

SECRETS

THE AUTHOR

Bernard MacLaverty was born in 1945 in Belfast, Northern Ireland, and studied English at Queen's University. He left Ireland in the early 1970s to live on Islay, an island in the Inner Hebrides off the west coast of Scotland. His first book, *Secrets and Other Stories* (from which this story is taken), won a Scottish Arts Council award in 1977. In 1980, his novel *Lamb* won the same award. *A Time to Dance and Other Stories* appeared in 1982, followed by the novel *Cal*, which deals directly with the political violence in Northern Ireland. Films have been made of both *Lamb* and *Cal*. Other books include *Walking the Dog and Other Stories* and *Grace Notes*.

THE STORY

Childhood is a state of constant exploration – pushing out the boundaries, asking questions, learning, understanding, not understanding, getting into trouble. Some lessons are painful to learn, and the pain lingers on into adulthood. 'A torn jacket is soon mended,' wrote the American poet Henry Longfellow; 'but hard words bruise the heart of a child.'

On her death bed great-aunt Mary is surrounded by her relatives, but she can no longer see or hear them. It is distressing to watch someone die, and for her great-nephew it becomes unbearable. He remembers her quiet dignity, remembers how as a child he sat on her knee while she read to him, remembers the unforgivable thing he once did . . .

SECRETS

He had been called to be there at the end. His great-aunt Mary had been dying for some days now and the house was full of relatives. He had just left his girlfriend's home – they had been studying for 'A' levels* together – and had come back to the house to find all the lights spilling on to the lawn and a sense of purpose which had been absent from the last few days.

He knelt at the bedroom door to join in the prayers. His knees were on the wooden threshold and he edged them forward on to the carpet. They had tried to wrap her fingers around a crucifix but they kept loosening. She lay low on the pillow and her face seemed to have shrunk by half since he had gone out earlier in the night. Her white hair was damped and pushed back from her forehead. She twisted her head from side to side, her eyes closed. The prayers chorused on, trying to cover the sound she was making deep in her throat. Someone said about her teeth and his mother leaned over her and said, 'That's the pet', and took her dentures from her mouth. The lower half of her face seemed to collapse. She half opened her eyes but could not raise her eyelids enough and showed only crescents of white.

'Hail Mary full of grace . . .' the prayers went on. He closed his hands over his face so that he would not have to look but smelt the trace of his girlfriend's handcream from his hands. The noise, deep and guttural, that his aunt was making became intolerable to him. It was as if she were drowning. She had lost all the dignity he knew her to have. He got up from the floor and stepped between the others who were kneeling and went into her sitting-room off the same landing.

He was trembling with anger or sorrow, he didn't know which. He sat in the brightness of her big sitting-room at the oval table and waited for something to happen. On the table was a cut-glass vase of irises, dying because she had been in bed for over a week. He sat staring at them. They were withering from the tips inward, scrolling themselves delicately, brown and neat. Clearing up after themselves. He stared at them for a long time until he heard the sounds of women weeping from the next room.

His aunt had been small – her head on a level with his when she sat at her table – and she seemed to get smaller each year. Her skin fresh, her hair white and waved and always well washed. She wore no jewelry except a cameo ring on the third finger of her right hand and, around her neck, a gold locket on a chain. The white classical profile on the ring was almost worn through and had become translucent and indistinct. The boy had noticed the ring when she had read to him as a child. In the beginning fairy tales, then as he got older extracts from famous novels, *Lorna Doone, Persuasion, Wuthering Heights* and her favourite extract, because she read it so often, Pip's meeting with Miss Havisham from *Great Expectations*. She would sit with him on her knee, her arms around him and holding the page flat with her hand. When he was bored he would interrupt her and ask about the ring. He loved hearing her tell of how her grandmother had given it to her as a brooch and she had had a ring made from it. He would try to count back to see how old it was. Had her grandmother got it from *her* grandmother? And if so, what had she turned it into? She would nod her head from side to side and say, 'How would I know a thing like that?' keeping her place in the closed book with her finger.

'Don't be so inquisitive,' she'd say. 'Let's see what happens next in the story.'

One day she was sitting copying figures into a long narrow book with a dip pen when he came into her room. She didn't look up, but when he asked her a question she just said, 'Mm?' and went on writing. The vase of irises on the oval table vibrated slightly as she wrote.

'What is it?' She wiped the nib on blotting-paper and looked up at him over her reading glasses.

'I've started collecting stamps and Mamma says you might have some.'

'Does she now—?'

She got up from the table and went to the tall walnut bureau-bookcase standing in the alcove. From a shelf of the bookcase she took a small wallet of keys and selected one for the lock. There was a harsh metal shearing sound as she pulled the desk flap down. The writing area was covered with green leather which had dog-eared at the corners. The inner part was divided into pigeon-holes, all bulging with papers. Some of them, envelopes, were gathered in batches nipped at the waist with elastic bands. There were postcards and bills and cash-books. She pointed to the postcards.

'You may have the stamps on those,' she said. 'But don't tear them. Steam them off.'

She went back to the oval table and continued writing. He sat on the arm of the chair, looking through the picture postcards – torchlight processions at Lourdes*, brown photographs of town centres, dull black and whites of beaches backed by faded hotels. Then he turned them over and began to sort the stamps. Spanish with a bald man, French with a rooster, German with funny jerky print, some Italian with what looked like a chimney-sweep's bundle and a hatchet.

'These are great,' he said. 'I haven't got any of them.'

'Just be careful how you take them off.'

'Can I take them downstairs?'

'Is your mother there?'

'Yes.'

'Then perhaps it's best if you bring the kettle up here.'

He went down to the kitchen. His mother was in the morning-room polishing silver. He took the kettle and the flex upstairs. Except for the dipping and scratching of his aunt's pen the room was silent. It was at the back of the house overlooking the orchard, and the sound of traffic from the main road was distant and muted. A tiny rattle began as the kettle warmed up, then it bubbled and steam gushed quietly from its spout. The cards began to curl slightly in the jet of steam, but she didn't seem to be watching. The stamps peeled moistly off and he put them in a saucer of water to flatten them.

'Who is Brother* Benignus?' he asked. She seemed not to hear. He asked again and she looked over her glasses.

'He was a friend.'

His flourishing signature appeared again and again. Sometimes Bro. Benignus, sometimes Benignus and once Iggy.

'Is he alive?'

'No, he's dead now. Watch the kettle doesn't run dry.'

When he had all the stamps off, he put the postcards together and replaced them in the pigeon-hole. He reached over towards the letters but before his hand touched them his aunt's voice, harsh for once, warned.

'A-a-a,' she moved her pen from side to side. 'Do-not-touch,' she said and smiled. 'Anything else, yes! That section, no!' She resumed her writing.

The boy went through some other papers and found some photographs. One was a beautiful girl. It was very old-fashioned but he could see that she was beautiful. The picture was a pale brown oval set on a white square of card. The edges of the oval were misty. The girl in the photograph was young and had dark, dark hair scraped severely back and tied like a knotted rope on the top of her head – high, arched eyebrows, her nose straight and thin;

her mouth slightly smiling, yet not smiling, the way a mouth is after smiling. Her eyes looked out at him, dark and knowing and beautiful.

'Who is that?' he asked.

'Why? What do you think of her?'

'She's all right.'

'Do you think she is beautiful?' The boy nodded.

'That's me,' she said. The boy was glad he had pleased her in return for the stamps.

Other photographs were there, not posed ones like Aunt Mary's but Brownie snaps* of laughing groups of girls in bucket hats like German helmets and coats to their ankles. They seemed tiny faces covered in clothes. There was a photograph of a young man smoking a cigarette, his hair combed one way by the wind against a background of sea.

'Who is that in the uniform?' the boy asked.

'He's a soldier,' she answered without looking up.

'Oh,' said the boy. 'But who is he?'

'He was a friend of mine before you were born,' she said; then added, 'Do I smell something cooking? Take your stamps and off you go. That's the boy.'

The boy looked at the back of the picture of the man and saw in black spidery ink 'John, Aug '15* Ballintoye'.

'I thought maybe it was Brother Benignus,' he said. She looked at him not answering.

'Was your friend killed in the war?'

At first she said no, but then she changed her mind.

'Perhaps he was,' she said, then smiled. 'You are far too inquisitive. Put it to use and go and see what is for tea. Your mother will need the kettle.' She came over to the bureau and helped tidy the photographs away. Then she locked it and put the keys on the shelf.

'Will you bring me up my tray?'

The boy nodded and left.

It was a Sunday evening, bright and summery. He was doing his homework and his mother was sitting on the carpet in one of her periodic fits of tidying out the drawers of the mahogany sideboard. On one side of her was a heap of paper scraps torn in quarters and bits of rubbish, on the other the useful items that had to be kept. The boy heard the bottom stair creak under Aunt Mary's light footstep. She knocked and put her head round the door and said that she was walking to Devotions. She was dressed in her good coat and hat and was just easing her fingers into her second glove. The boy saw her stop and pat her hair into place before the mirror in the hallway. His mother stretched over and slammed the door shut. It vibrated, then he heard the deeper sound of the outside door closing and her first few steps on the gravelled driveway. He sat for a long time wondering if he would have time or not. Devotions could take anything from twenty minutes to three quarters of an hour, depending on who was saying it.

Ten minutes must have passed, then the boy left his homework and went upstairs and into his aunt's sitting-room. He stood in front of the bureau wondering, then he reached for the keys. He tried several before he got the right one. The desk flap screeched as he pulled it down. He pretended to look at the postcards again in case there were any stamps he had missed. Then he put them away and reached for the bundle of letters. The elastic band was thick and old, brittle almost, and when he took it off its track remained on the wad of letters. He carefully opened one and took out the letter and unfolded it, frail, khaki-coloured.

My dearest Mary [it began] I am so tired I can hardly write to you. I have spent what seems like all day censoring letters (there is a howitzer about 100 yds away firing every 2 minutes). The letters are heart-rending in their attempt to express what they cannot. Some of the men are illiterate, others almost so. I know that they feel as much as we do, yet they do not have the words to express it. That is your job in the schoolroom, to give us generations who can read and write well. They have . . .

The boy's eye skipped down the page and over the next. He read the last paragraph.

Mary, I love you as much as ever – more so that we cannot be together. I do not know which is worse, the hurt of this war or being separated from you. Give all my love to Brendan and all at home.

It was signed, scribbled with what he took to be John. He folded the paper carefully into its original creases and put it in the envelope. He opened another.

My love, it is thinking of you that keeps me sane. When I get a moment I open my memories of you as if I were reading. Your long dark hair – I always imagine you wearing the blouse with the tiny roses, the white one that opened down the back – your eyes that said so much without words, the way you lowered your head when I said anything that embarrassed you, and the clean nape of your neck.

The day I think about most was the day we climbed the head at Ballycastle. In a hollow, out of the wind, the air full of pollen and the sound of insects, the grass warm and dry and you lying beside me, your hair undone, between me and the sun. You remember that that was where I first kissed you and the look of disbelief in your eyes that made me laugh afterwards.

It makes me laugh now to see myself savouring these memories standing alone up to my thighs in muck*. It is everywhere, two, three feet deep. To walk ten yards leaves you quite breathless.

I haven't time to write more today, so I leave you with my feet in the clay and my head in the clouds.

I love you, John.

He did not bother to put the letter back into the envelope but opened another.

My dearest, I am so cold that I find it difficult to keep my hand steady enough to write. You remember when we swam, the last two fingers of your hand went the colour and texture of candles with the cold. Well that is how I am all over. It is almost four days since I had any real sensation in my feet or legs. Everything is frozen. The ground is like steel.

Forgive me telling you this but I feel I have to say it to someone. The worst thing is the dead. They sit or lie frozen in the position they died. You can distinguish them from the living because their faces are the colour of slate. God help us when the thaw comes . . . This war is beginning to have an effect on me. I have lost all sense of feeling. The only emotion I have experienced lately is one of anger. Sheer white trembling anger. I have no pity or sorrow for the dead and injured. I thank God it is not me but I am enraged that it had to be them. If I live through this experience I will be a different person.

The only thing that remains constant is my love for you.

Today a man died beside me. A piece of shrapnel had pierced his neck as we were moving under fire. I pulled him into a crater and stayed with him until he died. I watched him choke and then drown in his blood.

I am full of anger which has no direction.

He sorted through the pile and read half of some, all of others. The sun had fallen low in the sky and shone directly into the room on to the pages he was reading, making the paper glare. He selected a letter from the back of the pile and shaded it with his hand as he read.

Dearest Mary, I am writing this to you from my hospital bed. I hope that you were not too worried about not hearing from me. I have been here, so they tell me, for two weeks, and it took another two weeks before I could bring myself to write this letter.

I have been thinking a lot as I lie here about the war and about myself and about you. I do not know how to say this but I feel deeply that I must do something, must sacrifice something to make up for the horror of the past year. In some strange way Christ has spoken to me through the carnage . . .

Suddenly the boy heard the creak of the stair and he frantically tried to slip the letter back into its envelope but it crumpled and would not fit. He bundled them all together. He could hear his aunt's familiar puffing on the short stairs to her room. He spread the elastic band wide with his fingers. It snapped and the letters scattered. He pushed them into their pigeon-hole and quickly closed the desk flap. The brass screeched loudly and clicked shut. At that moment his aunt came into the room.

'What are you doing, boy?' she snapped.

'Nothing.' He stood with the keys in his hand. She walked to the bureau and opened it. The letters sprung out in an untidy heap.

'You have been reading my letters,' she said quietly. Her mouth was tight with the words and her eyes blazed. The boy could say nothing. She struck him across the side of the face.

'Get out,' she said. 'Get out of my room.'

The boy, the side of his face stinging and red, put the keys on the table on his way out. When he reached the door she called to him. He stopped, his hand on the handle.

'You are dirt,' she hissed, 'and always will be dirt. I shall remember this till the day I die.'

Even though it was a warm evening, there was a fire in the large fireplace. His mother had asked him to light it so that she could clear out Aunt Mary's stuff. The room could then be his study, she said. She came in and seeing him at the table said, 'I hope I'm not disturbing you.'

'No.'

She took the keys from her pocket, opened the bureau and began burning papers and cards. She glanced quickly at each one before she flicked it on to the fire.

'Who was Brother Benignus?' he asked.

His mother stopped sorting and said, 'I don't know. Your aunt kept herself very much to herself. She got books from him through the post occasionally. That much I do know.'

She went on burning the cards. They built into strata, glowing red and black. Now and again she broke up the pile with the poker, sending showers of sparks up the chimney. He saw her come to the letters. She took off the elastic band and put it to one side with the useful things and began dealing the envelopes into the fire. She opened one and read quickly through it, then threw it on top of the burning pile.

'Mama,' he said.

'Yes?'

'Did Aunt Mary say anything about me?'

'What do you mean?'

'Before she died – did she say anything?'

'Not that I know of – the poor thing was too far gone to speak,

God rest her.' She went on burning, lifting the corners of the letters with the poker to let the flames underneath them.

When he felt a hardness in his throat, he put his head down on his books. Tears came into his eyes for the first time since she had died, and he cried silently into the crook of his arm for the woman who had been his maiden aunt, his teller of tales, that she might forgive him.

NOTES

'A' levels (p110)

a British exam (Advanced level) taken in a particular subject, usually in the final year of school at the age of 18

Lourdes (p112)

a town in south-west France, where miraculous healings are said to take place, and which is a major centre of pilgrimage for Christians

Brother (p113)

a man who has entered a Roman Catholic religious community and become a monk (monks are not allowed to marry)

Brownie snaps (p114)

photographs taken by a 'Brownie' camera, a simple box camera popular in the 1950s

'15 (p114)

short for the year 1915; so the war referred to here is the First World War, 1914–1918

muck (p117)

mud; the trenches in the battlefields of the First World War were notorious for their mud

DISCUSSION

1 When Aunt Mary finds the boy reading her private letters, she hits him across the face and calls him 'dirt'. Do you think this was a justifiable reaction? What would *you* do or say in a similar situation?

2 It seems that the years passed without either Aunt Mary or the boy referring to the matter again, or telling anyone else (for example, the boy's mother) about it. Was this the best thing to do? What, in your opinion, should Aunt Mary or the boy have done next?

3 In one of the letters to Mary, John wrote that he felt he 'must sacrifice something'. What did he mean by this? And what clues are we given in the story as to Mary's reaction to this 'sacrifice'?

4 What impression did you form of Brother Benignus? What kind of man was he? How did he change?

5 Did you find this a moving story? Who did you feel greater sympathy for – Aunt Mary or the boy? Why?

LANGUAGE FOCUS

1 When the boy asks Aunt Mary if her friend was killed in the war, at first she says no, then changes her mind and says, 'Perhaps he was.' Because of what we know of her history, these three words carry a great weight of meaning. What words might Aunt Mary have used if she had explained her meaning in full?

2 Aunt Mary expresses her anger to the boy with these words:

You are dirt, and always will be dirt. I shall remember this till the day I die.

Do you think calling someone 'dirt' is a very hurtful thing to say? What other expressions of anger can you think of, to express your opinion of someone who has done a despicable thing? Are they stronger or milder than 'You are dirt'? Put all your expressions in a list, and decide which you could say (in the appropriate circumstances)

a) to a child
b) to an adult you don't know very well
c) to an adult you know very well.

ACTIVITIES

1 Suppose that the boy went to his mother after the incident with Aunt Mary's letters, and that the boy's mother knew all about Brother Benignus and what had happened during and after the war. Imagine you are the boy's mother and tell the boy Aunt Mary's story in as clear and simple a way as possible.

2 If the boy had talked to his mother, perhaps she would have advised him to write a note of apology to his aunt. Would such an apology be best kept short and simple, just confessing the wrongdoing and asking for forgiveness, or should the boy try to explain why he did it? Write the boy's apology for him.

3 How do you think Mary felt when she read John's letter and realized what 'sacrifice' he was talking about? Was she angry, sad, heart-broken, forgiving, bewildered, understanding – or all of these at the same time? Write her diary entry for that day, as she tries to come to terms with her changed future. (Remember that there was still at that point a strong chance that John might have been killed before the war ended.)

THE LICENCE

THE AUTHOR

Frank Tuohy, of Irish and Scottish origins, was born in England in 1925. He was educated at Stowe School and King's College, Cambridge, and lived for extended periods in Japan, Poland, Argentina, Portugal, and the United States, where he taught at Purdue University. He wrote three novels, three books of short stories, and an illustrated biography of the Irish poet W. B. Yeats. He won several literary awards, including the James Tait Black Memorial Prize in 1964 for his novel *The Ice Saints*. His short stories, which appeared in collections entitled *The Admiral and the Nuns, Fingers in the Door and Other Stories*, and *Live Bait and Other Stories*, have been praised for their elegance, wit, and quiet subtlety. Tuohy died in April 1999.

THE STORY

Adolescence is an awkward time. You are no longer a child and not quite an adult, but are poised uncertainly on the brink of both worlds. You don't want to be treated as a child, but your changed status seems often to be ignored by those around you. And the adult world, though full of enticing new freedoms, is not always a comfortable place to be. In other words, as an adolescent, you can't win.

Perhaps the best thing is to say as little as possible. Peter, intent on having driving-lessons and acquiring his licence, keeps a close guard over his tongue. He has a lot to cope with in his life: the recent death of his mother, a fussing aunt, his father's inadequacies – and his father's new housekeeper, the menacing Mrs Macdonnell . . .

The Licence

Aunt Cynthia rarely made personal use of the chairs in her London drawing-room. She was kneeling now on the hearth rug, and poking at the grate from time to time with a pair of tongs. When she turned round, her face would be full of endeavour at sympathy and understanding. It is a great effort to talk to boys of Peter's age.

Awkwardly waiting for her to speak again, he looked as if he might break the chair he was sitting in.

'Does your father write to you?'

'Yes, of course.'

'Often?'

'Yes.' Adolescence still made Peter's voice thrum like a slack guitar string. 'At school we're meant to write home every week, so, as I usually do, he pretty well has to; I mean he writes something, not much though.'

His aunt struck a heated coal and it split satisfactorily, emitting branches of flame. 'What does he write about?'

Peter laughed oafishly. 'About my future mostly.'

'Surely that can wait. What about himself? Has he told you any plans?'

'We're going to Austria this summer. He wants me to learn to drive.'

'You're too young.'

'I won't be then.' He laughed again, to help things on.

She was agitated and fussed. The boy had a train to catch in half an hour's time. Though partly impelled by curiosity, her sympathy was genuine; but he deflected it at every opportunity.

'Please don't always try to shut me out, Peter.'

He looked at her with hatred and desperation.

'I suppose it isn't any use. You're just a child.'

Her husband, a barrister, came in with the evening papers.

'Hullo, Pete, old boy.'

'Hullo, Uncle Raymond.'

Raymond Pelham issued a big grin: everybody felt they had to start off cheerfully with Peter.

'Darling, Carla's been pressing your dinner jacket. Do go and see if it's all right.'

'What did she want to do that for?'

'Because we're dining at the Messiters. Darling, please.'

'I expect it's all right. Is Pete old enough to have a glass of sherry?'

'Darling, please,' Aunt Cynthia went on signalling until her husband left the room, first winking at Peter on the way.

She put a hand on Peter's knee.

'This housekeeper, Mrs What's-her-name.'

'Mrs Macdonnell.'

'Yes. What does your father write about her?'

'Nothing much. Why?'

His aunt turned back to the fire, armed this time with the poker.

'He got her from an agency,' Peter said, trying to help.

'Oh, God. How difficult it is!' Aunt Cynthia hit a smoking coal with some violence, but it failed to crumble. 'He's my favourite brother. I was fond of your mother too. She could be a very very sweet person.'

At this, Peter was locked in silence.

'You'd better go to your train. I'll ring the taxi rank.'

'I can go by tube.'

'With your squash racket and record-player and everything?'

'Oh, all right.'

In the hall, they listened for the taxi. When they heard it stop outside, Aunt Cynthia kissed him. He still reeked of boarding school, as men do of prison; in her arms he held himself quite still, like an animal tense and ready to leap away at the first relaxation. She let him go, with a hurt little laugh.

Afterwards she said to her husband: 'I sometimes think he hates me.'

'He probably still feels like hell, poor Pete.'

'That's no answer. It's five months now – I was counting this morning.'

She moved into his arms. Raymond knew that for her the problem was, not Peter, but her own childlessness.

Because his father had evening surgery, Peter could not be met at Shereham station. He took another taxi to the house, which lay a mile away, among bird-haunted shrubberies. The drive spat and crackled with new gravel.

'There he is at last! I expect you know who I am, don't you?'

The woman in the doorway spoke in a soft Edinburgh voice. She was about forty, and wore a knitted suit and her dark hair done up in a bun. On her bright, bird-like face, the lips were thin and scarlet.

Peter dropped his squash racket to shake hands.

'I'm Mrs Macdonnell. When you've got over your first shyness, I expect you'll want to call me Helen. Come along up, then.'

Peter picked up his bags again and made off up the stairs, with Mrs Macdonnell following him.

'There's a big strong laddie.'

The room was small, on the sunless side of the house, a museum of Peter's past. He put his record-player and a case of records on the bed.

'Those'll be all the latest smash-hits.'

'No,' Peter said.

'What are they then? Dixieland*?' She was showing him she knew all the modern words.

'Bach* mostly.'

'Gloomy stuff, eh? Well, I never.'

She seemed put out, and left him, shaking her head as though she knew he'd be growing out of this phase. 'You'll be coming down when you're ready.'

Peter's trunk would arrive later. He unpacked his suitcase quickly and put the clothes in the drawer; if he left it, she might do it for him. He hid under his handkerchiefs the photograph of his mother, and the letter she had written to him before she died.

Dr Hesketh was standing in front of the drawing-room fire with a whisky and soda. He had reddish hair, which was growing colourless, and a bristly moustache. He always looked ruffled and embarrassed; everyone over the past few months had conspired to expect too much of him.

Peter and his father shook hands. It was, nowadays, their only way of touching, and they hardly glanced at each other.

Mrs Macdonnell said: 'You know I think he's got quite a look of you, Jack. Quite a look.'

At the sound of his father's Christian name, Peter flinched visibly. His father stared at the logs in the grate.

'He's taller, though. The wee bairn's* taller than his daddy.' She drained her sherry. 'Well, then, I'll be going through to get you your supper. I expect you two have lots to talk about.'

Relieved of her presence, they could talk to each other quite easily.

'Aunt Cynthia's got seats for Covent Garden* next week. She wants me to go up.'

'You go then. It's no fun for you now, moping around down here.'

'Have you thought any more about my driving lessons?'

'Yes, I don't see why you shouldn't begin as soon as you can.'

'Mr Beaman – he's the history master – let me practise stopping and starting in his Mini*. In the school grounds, so I didn't need a licence.'

'Well then, you know the rudiments.'

'Yes.'

Both Peter and his father knew they would over-discuss this subject: they exploited to the utmost the few topics for conversation that now remained to them.

Mrs Macdonnell called them.

'Not much for supper, I'm afraid. Today's the day I have my hair done.'

His father ate in silence, pouring tomato ketchup onto the thawed-out fishcakes. When they had finished, he whispered to Peter: 'Give her a hand with the dishes, there's a good lad.'

He went through to the kitchen.

'That's nice of you, Peter. I see they look after your manners at that school, not like some of these places.'

Peter seized a cloth and began drying plates strenuously.

'How do you think Dad is looking?'

He did not answer.

'Lost your tongue, have you? Never mind. As I say, you'll soon get over your shyness with Helen.'

'Actually, I call him Pa.'

She laughed, 'Do you now? Old-fashioned, aren't we?'

'He's all right, I suppose.'

Mrs Macdonnell put down the dish-mop. 'Your father's a fine good man, Peter. He wears himself out for those patients of his, but they're not grateful, not a bit of it.'

She poured bleach into the basin.

'They don't know they're lucky. I was an ill woman when I came here, Peter. You're not old enough to know about these things. Your father's been a trump to me, a real trump.'

She unbuttoned her apron. Her sentimentality was full of menace.

'There's not many like him, these days. People down here don't know they're well off. And all these foreigners that work at the big

houses! – They're not healthy, you know. I wouldn't have one of
them in my house. And they don't do the work, either.'

Peter ducked away as soon as he could. Upstairs he lay flat on his
bed, and put a Haydn* quartet on the record-player. A few minutes
later she was at his door.

'D'ye like the sound o' the pipes, Peter? D'ye no like the sound
of the good Scots pipes?'

'I don't know much about them,' he said politely.

'There's nothing to beat them.'

She gave no signs of going away. Soon she tried whistling and
humming a bit, to help Haydn along; it was the allegretto*, however,
and he was too quick for her.

'What do you have, Peter?'

'What?'

'What! Did ye never learn to say "pardon"? What'll you be having
for your nightcap? Will it be Horlick's or Ovaltine* or cocoa or hot
milk?'

'Nothing, thank you.'

'Ah, come now. Not even a nice cup of tea? Won't you join Helen
in a nice cup of tea? She always has one, this time o' nights.'

'No, thank you.'

Huffed, she finally went away. Peter raised the arm of the pickup
and put it back to where it had been when she first came in.

Later Peter stayed awake, listening. But the silence in the house
was absolute. There was only a faint ringing sound out of the spring
darkness, which might have been the blood encircling the walls of
his own brain.

And then across the corridor, a small regular noise: Mrs
Macdonnell snoring. A guileless innocent murmur, it seemed to fill
the whole house until Peter went to sleep.

ᔥ

Coming out of his bedroom, where he had been rearranging his long-playing records, Peter bumped into a small grey figure armed with a feather mop.

'They never tell me you was back! How are you then, dear?'

'I'm fine, Mrs Parkes. How are things?'

'Oh, it's not the same.' The old woman's eyes sparkled with grief and mischief. 'It's not the same by a long chalk.'

Mrs Macdonnell called upstairs: 'Mrs Parkes, I've left the vacuum cleaner out, so's you can give downstairs a proper doing today.'

Mrs Parkes made a face at Peter. 'See what I mean? Only I'm loyal, see? I won't let Doctor down. I said that to your poor mother, I won't let Doctor down.'

Relishing this, she was going to repeat it, but Mrs Macdonnell had come half-way up the stairs, her head raised, scenting trouble.

'Your father's just off, Peter, once I've made his list out. You're going with him, aren't you?'

'Oh, all right.'

Dr Hesketh was downstairs drinking a cup of tea. Mrs Macdonnell stood dutifully beside him with his list. She gave Peter a little smile, which indicated the regularity and reliability of this event.

Peter's father pointed to one name. 'Who's that?'

'I can't spell the foreign names, Jack. It's that cook at Shereham Hall.'

'Right ho. Nothing going to hold us up for long there.' He pocketed his stethoscope.

'Now, boys, don't you go being late for lunch. One o'clock sharp, mind.'

Peter followed his father out to the garage.

'It's probably only corned beef, anyway,' his father said, starting the car. Peter giggled.

The houses round Shereham were bright with new paint and daffodils and pink cherry-trees were in flower in the easily run gardens.

On the few remaining bits of pasture, horses and ponies which belonged to the daughters of London businessmen were frisking in the sunshine. Dr Hesketh visited two or three council houses and a thatched cottage, in which a family waited for a grandmother to die: they had already an offer from London people. Sometimes he stopped for a moment behind the car, out of sight of the windows. He came out of the last cottage whistling, and drove to Shereham Hall.

'Got something to read, old man? I may be a bit of time here.'

'Is the cook very ill?'

'No, not really. Be a bit of time, though.'

Shereham Hall was a square Palladian mansion built of pale sandstone. In the Portico there were croquet mallets, and some hooded basket-chairs. The garden was very large and would soon be opened to the public, in aid of the District Nurses.

After half an hour, there were voices, especially his father's, which sounded louder than before. Mr and Mrs Tyrell Bailey, both with pale hair and long whey-coloured faces, came out with him.

Mrs Tyrell Bailey leaned towards the car. 'So this is the boy.'

'Oh yes, the boy,' Mr Tyrell Bailey said.

Peter was trapped, like a fish under observation in an aquarium, but before he could get out of the car, they had lost interest in him. With the slow saunter of garden-viewers, they had crossed the drive and were approaching a large magnolia tree, which stood in full blossom near the lake. Mrs Tyrell Bailey was telling his father about the tree, and his father was nodding a great many times.

After a few minutes Peter's father returned across the lawn, smiling to himself and mopping his hands with a handkerchief. He got into the car in silence. As a child Peter had once said to his mother: 'Pa smells like the cocktail cabinet.' This joke had not been funny a second time.

'Well, off we go.'

Gravel roared under the tyres, Shereham Hall, the basket chairs and the magnolia tree spun round, and the car raced towards a wall of rhododendrons. Beside the lake, the faces of the Tyrell Baileys flashed by, identically aghast. The car reached the bottom of the drive, swooped into the main road, and came to a halt.

'Get out, get out, you little fool,' Dr Hesketh shouted. 'See what it is.'

Peter scrambled out and ran to the front of the car.

A schoolboy, several years younger than himself, was kneeling on his hands and knees in the road. The wheels of his bicycle were still spinning furiously.

'Are you all right?'

The boy got up. He wore shorts and a county school cap, and his overfed face was white with fear. His smooth knees were grazed and the palms of his hands pitted with the marks of stones.

'I think . . .' Tame, neuter-looking, he was ready to apologize. 'P'raps I should've rung my bell.'

'Are you sure you're all right? My father's a doctor, he could probably help.'

'No, I'm all right.' Nearly crying, the boy wanted to be left to himself.

Peter rummaged in his pocket and produced five shillings. 'Here, take this.'

Startled, the boy said, 'Thank you, sir,' and they both blushed. He picked up his bicycle, spun the pedals once or twice, then mounted and wobbled slowly away up the hill. Peter watched him until he had disappeared round a corner.

In the car Peter's father was leaning forward with forehead resting on the top of the steering wheel.

Peter sat beside him in silence.

'Sorry, Pete. Sometimes, I can't see things – I can't—'

'Let's stay here a bit.'

His father leaned back, showing that his cheeks were wet. 'No, better get back. Helen'll be waiting lunch.' He took out a cigarette with violently trembling hands. Peter pulled out the dashboard lighter to help him.

'Now, you see, Pete, why you'd better learn to drive.'

'I want to, anyway.'

'Peter, you'd better know about this. I've been under a lot of strain lately. Very private strain.'

The expression sounded peculiar. After a moment he inquired cautiously: 'Is it about Ma?'

'No, it isn't.'

'Oh,' Peter said.

Late that night Peter heard somebody moving about the house. Without thinking, he put on his dressing-gown and crept to the end of the corridor. Mrs Macdonnell was standing at the top of the stairs. Wearing no make-up, with her hair hanging in two long dark braids down her frilly white night-dress, she looked both archaic and sexy, like somebody out of the Brontës*.

'Who is it?'

'Hesketh. I mean, Peter.'

'Must I be always after you two laddies? Somebody left the light on in the hallway.'

He shivered, clutching his shrunken fawn dressing-gown – someone at school had pinched the cord years ago. His large greyish feet were cold on the floorboards. She came closer to him.

'Off to bed with you now.'

Her eyes were an entire shock: they were hard with hatred, like little darts of steel. He turned and without dignity made his way back to his room. She was watching him the whole time, and his hair prickled and his skin crawled.

'So you're off today, are you, dear?' Mrs Parkes said. Peter was wearing his London suit. 'Well, I can't say I blame you. That auntie of yours, Mrs Pelham, she's a kind soul. She spoke quite nicely to me after the funeral. I told her I'd stick with Doctor, and I done it up to now. But this isn't a happy house. You're well out of it.'

Peter's provisional driving licence had arrived by the morning's post. He showed it to his father at breakfast.

'Good man. I'll fix up those driving lessons before you come back. You may as well have something to do in the last week of the holidays.'

'Do you think I'll be able to drive in Austria?'

'I don't see why not.' His father was silent, buttering a piece of toast. 'It probably won't be Austria, in fact. Helen thinks she'd prefer Switzerland.'

Their eyes failed to meet across the tablecloth.

'Oh, I see.'

When they had both finished, Peter stacked the breakfast things and carried them through to the kitchen. Mrs Macdonnell was standing at the sink, doing the flowers.

'Well, you're off now, are you, Peter? No doubt that aunt of yours will be spoiling you again. Funny, I thought you were a nice polite boy, first of all. Well, we live and learn and that's our misfortune.'

She cut through the stalks of a bunch of jonquils; they fell stickily, one by one.

'No, don't go yet. Listen to me a moment, Peter.' Her voice dropped. 'Now, young feller me lad, don't you be talking out of turn. No telling tales out of school, got it? Because if you do, laddie, you'll live to regret it. You'll live to regret it very much. Helen can be real nasty, when she's the mind to it. And one thing she doesn't take to is dirty little sneaking eavesdroppers. There's your daddy calling. Now remember what I said.'

Peter got into the car beside his father.

'I'll ring up about the lessons today. And you can start driving me around for practice.'

Peter did not answer. His father accepted this, and looked straight ahead, his face twitching with guilt.

Cynthia Pelham had been taking Peter out to lunch.

She had made an immense effort to stop making remarks like 'I suppose it's no use suggesting you do something about your hair?' She had refrained from straightening him up altogether, apart from insisting he got his shoes cleaned by the man on the corner of Piccadilly Circus. He bought the clothes he wanted, including two frightful ties. In the restaurant she had let him order what he liked, and allowed him, with certain afterthoughts, to drink a glass of wine. Now she pushed money under the table at him, whispering: 'The man pays.'

'It's obvious you're paying,' Peter said. 'The waiters all know.'

They returned home exhausted.

Tea was waiting and with it, by prearrangement, was Juliet, Cynthia's oldest friend.

'Washing his hands.'

'How are things?' Juliet asked.

'Worse, if anything. Of course, I scrupulously refrain from mentioning, and all that. But really, it's been half a year now. And it isn't as if everything between Jack and Elizabeth had been so absolutely marvellous, because I happen to know—'

'What on earth difference should that make to Peter?'

'No, none, I suppose.' Cynthia sighed. 'I'm sorry, darling, I'm tired. He'll be down in a minute. Try a spot of charm, will you?'

'I'm sure he's a perfectly normal boy,' Juliet said. 'It's just that—'

'It's just that he's going through a phase. I know. Jolly long phase. I wonder if a psychiatrist—'

'I'd leave him alone if I were you.'

Kneeling on the rug, Cynthia bit into a piece of bread and butter. 'Nobody helps.'

'Honestly, I'd skip it. What good bread you always have – though of course I shouldn't be eating it.'

'He's impossible.'

'I can remember when everyone said "Cynthia's impossible".'

Peter's aunt blushed a little. 'You know perfectly well that was about something quite different.'

The stairs shook overhead and the pictures began rattling.

'Peter, darling, come and have some tea.' His aunt had not called him 'darling' before, and this embarrassed both herself and him.

He shook hands with Juliet and sat down. Fair and gleaming and beautifully dressed, the two women filled the immediate view. They tried to talk about Covent Garden, but since Peter was the only one of them with any knowledge of opera, conversation did not progress. Juliet had been to Glyndebourne* three or four times, but couldn't remember any of the names.

'When do you go back?' she asked him. 'I'm sorry, I don't mean school – I know everybody always asks that. I meant to Shereham.'

'The day after tomorrow.'

'So soon!'

'Peter's having driving lessons,' Aunt Cynthia said.

'Yes?'

'My father wants me to drive when we go on holiday. We're going to Austria.' He stopped, then continued: 'At least, I mean, Switzerland. Also he wants me to drive him when he visits patients.'

To Juliet, Cynthia made a tiny elbow-lifting gesture, which Peter observed.

'I think that's marvellous,' Juliet said. 'Your father will be pleased. How's he getting on with his new housekeeper?'

Peter stared at the floor between his feet. 'She does her job.'

Cynthia, collecting the teacups, muttered: 'Yes, but what job, that's what we'd all like to know.'

Peter got up and walked out of the room.

'Darling!' Juliet said.

'Have I said something awful?'

'Yes, you have.'

Cynthia went scarlet. 'Well, everything one says is awful. It's absolute hell, you don't know what I've been through.'

This evening Peter's father was waiting for him at Shereham Station.

'Hullo, old boy. Got your luggage?'

'Yes.'

'How's Aunt Cynthia?'

'She's all right,' Peter said. 'She sent you her love.'

He handed in his ticket and followed his father into the car park.

'Not too tired after all your junketings?'

'No, of course not. Why?'

'I thought of going over for a bite at the Ram at Chillington. They do quite a decent meal there. It's outside my parish, so there's no risk of meeting patients. We used to go there a lot in the old days.'

'That'd be lovely.'

'Mrs Parkes has been leaving me something in the oven, but I told her not to bother tonight, as you were coming down.'

His father spoke excitedly and rather fast, and Peter had to wait until they got into the car before asking: 'Where's Mrs Macdonnell?'

His father was silent a moment. 'I – I gave her the sack. We had a bit of a bust up, so I said she could leave at once. Come, now, her cooking wasn't so fancy, was it?'

Peter giggled. 'It certainly wasn't.'

His father drove very slowly through Shereham and swerved out onto the dark Chillington road.

'Pa, can I have wine at dinner?'

'Well, that's not really the object of the exercise, but I should think so. In moderation.'

A minute or two later his father drew up at the roadside.

'Got your licence on you?'

'Yes, I have.'

'Like to drive?'

'Yes, I would.'

'Good man. Hop out then, and I'll move over.'

Peter let in the clutch perfectly and the car slid off towards Chillington.

Notes

Dixieland (p126)
   a kind of jazz music
Bach (p126)
   a famous German composer of classical music
wee bairn (p127)
   Scottish dialect words for 'small child'
Covent Garden (p127)
   the name of a famous opera house in London
Mini (p127)
   the model name of a small British car, popular in the 1960s
Haydn (p129)
   a famous Austrian composer of classical music
allegretto (p129)
   a musical term (Italian) meaning a passage played at a brisk tempo
Horlick's, Ovaltine (p129)
   proprietary names of drinks made with hot milk
Brontës (p133)
   The three Brontë sisters (Charlotte, Emily, and Anne) are famous
   nineteenth-century English novelists
Glyndebourne (p136)
   a country house in the south of England, where a festival of opera is
   held every year

Discussion

1 How did the various characters in the story treat Peter – as a child, as
   an adult, or as something in between? Describe the different attitudes
   of Aunt Cynthia, Peter's father, Mrs Macdonnell, and the boy on the
   bicycle at Shereham Hall. Do you think Peter's own behaviour
   influenced their attitudes? If so, how?

2 Which character did you feel most sympathy for? Why?

3 What is the significance of the driving licence? Why do you think the
   author made it the title of the story?

Language Focus

1 The accident at Shereham Hall is described in a series of breathless
   phrases, as though representing the shock and suddenness of the event

as experienced by Peter. The Tyrell Baileys witnessed the whole thing from beside the lake, their faces 'identically aghast'. Write a description of the accident from their point of view, filling in the details to give a clear account of what happened.

2 Rephrase these expressions from the story in your own words.
   Please don't always try to shut me out   (p124)
   She seemed put out   (p127)
   Lost your tongue, have you?   (p128)
   He wears himself out for those patients of his   (p128)
   Your father's been a trump to me, a real trump   (p128)
   It's not the same by a long chalk   (p130)
   I won't let Doctor down   (p130)
   You're well out of it   (p134)
   Don't you be talking out of turn   (p134)
   I gave her the sack   (p137)
   We had a bit of a bust up   (p137)

3 Several times Peter chose to remain silent, rather than speak – or perhaps he couldn't find the right words to express himself. Find the following five occasions in the text, and invent responses for Peter, which you feel reflect what he might have been feeling at that moment.
   • *At this, Peter was locked in silence.*   (p125)
   • *At the sound of his father's Christian name, Peter flinched visibly.* (p127)
   • *'How do you think Dad is looking?' He did not answer.*   (p128)
   • *Peter sat beside him in silence.*   (p132)
   • *Peter did not answer. His father accepted this, and looked straight ahead, his face twitching with guilt.*   (p135)

ACTIVITIES

1 Perhaps Peter phones his aunt to tell her that Mrs Macdonnell has gone. Write their conversation, with Aunt Cynthia pressing to find out as much as possible, and Peter saying as little as he can.

2 With Mrs Macdonnell gone, might Peter and his father have a better chance of getting on together? Have all the problems now disappeared? Write a new ending for the story, describing briefly how the rest of Peter's holidays passed, with the driving lessons and the trip to Austria.

THE RUNAWAY

THE AUTHOR

Morley Callaghan was born in 1903 in Toronto, Canada. He attended the University of Toronto, followed by law school, but began to write seriously in 1923. As a reporter on the Toronto *Star* he met Ernest Hemingway, who encouraged him to publish his first novel, *Strange Fugitive*. Other novels include *They Shall Inherit the Earth, The Many Colored Coat, A Passion in Rome*, and *A Fine and Private Place*. His tight, economical prose is shown to best advantage in his collections of short stories, *A Native Argosy, No Man's Meat, Now That April's Here, Morley Callaghan Stories*, and *Lost and Found Stories*. Callaghan died in Toronto in 1990.

THE STORY

Young people can sometimes be very sensitive, perhaps too sensitive. They brood on small failings until they are magnified into something dreadful. A quarrel assumes a significance out of all proportion; a feeling of discontent can become a cosmic gloom. Nobody understands what they are going through; nobody in the universe has ever felt like this before.

Michael is a boy in some ways, a young man in others. He does boy-like things with his friends, and agonizes over the tensions at home between his father and stepmother. He longs to impress the girl of his dreams, but can't find the right words to talk to her. Nothing in his life seems quite right; there is only one solution . . .

THE RUNAWAY

In the lumber-yard by the lake there was an old brick building two storeys high and all around the foundations were heaped great piles of soft sawdust, softer than the thick moss in the woods. There were many of these golden mounds of dust covering that part of the yard right down to the blue lake. That afternoon all the fellows followed Michael up the ladder to the roof of the old building and they sat with their legs hanging over the edge looking out at the whitecaps on the water. Michael was younger than some of them but he was much bigger, his legs were long, his huge hands dangled awkwardly at his sides and his thick black hair curled up all over his head. 'I'll stump you all to jump down,' he said suddenly, and without thinking about it, he shoved himself off the roof and fell on the sawdust where he lay rolling around and laughing.

'You're all stumped,' he shouted, 'You're all yellow,' he said, coaxing them to follow him. Still laughing, he watched them looking down from the roof white-faced and hesitant, and then one by one they jumped and got up grinning with relief.

In the hot afternoon sunlight they all lay on the sawdust pile telling jokes till at last one of the fellows said, 'Come on up on the old roof again and jump down.' There wasn't much enthusiasm among them, but they all went up to the roof again and began to jump off in a determined, desperate way till only Michael was left and the others were all down below grinning up at him and calling, 'Come on, Mike. What's the matter with you?' Michael longed to jump down there and be with them, but he remained on the edge of the roof wetting his lips, with a silly grin on his face, wondering why it had not seemed such a long drop the first time. For a while they thought he was only kidding them, then they saw him clenching his fists. He was trying to count to ten and then jump, and when that failed, he tried to take a long breath and close his eyes.

In a while the fellows began to jeer at him; they were tired of waiting and it was getting on to dinner-time. 'Come on, you're yellow, do you think we're going to sit here all night?' they began to shout, and when he did not move they began to get up and walk away, still jeering. 'Who did this in the first place? What's the matter with you guys?' he shouted.

But for a long time he remained on the edge of the roof, staring unhappily and steadily at the ground. He remained all alone for nearly an hour while the sun like a great orange ball getting bigger and bigger rolled slowly over the gray line beyond the lake. His clothes were wet from nervous sweating. At last he closed his eyes, slipped off the roof, fell heavily on the pile of sawdust and lay there a long time. There were no sounds in the yard, the workmen had gone home. As he lay there he wondered why he had been unable to move; and then he got up slowly and walked home feeling deeply ashamed and wanting to avoid everybody.

He was so late for dinner that his stepmother said to him sarcastically, 'You're big enough by this time surely to be able to get home in time for dinner. But if you won't come home, you'd better try staying in tonight.' She was a well-built woman with a fair, soft skin and a little touch of gray in her hair and an eternally patient smile on her face. She was speaking now with a restrained, passionless severity, but Michael, with his dark face gloomy and sullen, hardly heard her; he was still seeing the row of grinning faces down below on the sawdust pile and hearing them jeer at him.

As he ate his cold dinner he was rolling his brown eyes fiercely and sometimes shaking his big black head. His father, who was sitting in the armchair by the window, a huge man with his hair nearly all gone so that his smooth wide forehead rose in a beautiful shining dome, kept looking at him steadily. When Michael had finished eating and had gone out to the veranda, his father followed, sat down beside him, lit his pipe and said gently, 'What's bothering you, son?'

'Nothing, Dad. There's nothing bothering me,' Michael said, but he kept on staring out at the gray dust drifting off the road.

His father kept coaxing and whispering in a voice that was amazingly soft for such a big man. As he talked, his long fingers played with the heavy gold watch fob on his vest. He was talking about nothing in particular and yet by the tone of his voice he was expressing a marvellous deep friendliness that somehow seemed to become a part of the twilight and then of the darkness. And Michael began to like the sound of his father's voice, and soon he blurted out, 'I guess by this time all the guys around here are saying I'm yellow. I'd like to be a thousand miles away.' He told how he could not force himself to jump off the roof the second time. But his father lay back in the armchair laughing in that hearty, rolling, easy way that Michael loved to hear; years ago when Michael had been younger and he was walking along the paths in the evening, he used to try and laugh like his father only his voice was not deep enough and he would grin sheepishly and look up at the trees overhanging the paths as if someone hiding up there had heard him. 'You'll be all right with the bunch, son,' his father was saying. 'I'm betting you'll lick any boy in town that says you're yellow.'

But there was the sound of the screen door opening, and Michael's stepmother said in her mild, firm way, 'If I've rebuked the boy, Henry, as I think he ought to be rebuked, I don't know why you should be humouring him.'

'You surely don't object to me talking to Michael.'

'I simply want you to be reasonable, Henry.'

In his grave, unhurried way Mr Lount got up and followed his wife into the house and soon Michael could hear them arguing; he could hear his father's firm, patient voice floating clearly out to the street; then his stepmother's voice, mild at first, rising, becoming hysterical till at last she cried out wildly, 'You're setting the boy against me. You don't want him to think of me as his mother. The two of you are against me. I know your nature.'

As he looked up and down the street fearfully, Michael began to make prayers that no one would pass by who would think, 'Mr and Mrs Lount are quarrelling again.' Alert, he listened for faint sounds on the cinder path, but he heard only the frogs croaking under the bridge opposite Stevenson's place and the far-away cry of a freight train passing behind the hills. 'Why did Dad have to get married? It used to be swell on the farm,' he thought, remembering how he and his father had gone fishing down at the glen. And then while he listened to the sound of her voice, he kept thinking that his stepmother was a fine woman, only she always made him uneasy because she wanted him to like her, and then when she found out that he couldn't think of her as his mother, she had grown resentful. 'I like her and I like my father. I don't know why they quarrel. They're really such fine people. Maybe it's because Dad shouldn't have sold the farm and moved here. There's nothing for him to do.' Unable to get interested in the town life, his father loafed all day down at the hotel or in Bailey's flour-and-feed store but he was such a fine-looking, dignified, reticent man that the loafers would not accept him as a crony. Inside the house now, Mrs Lount was crying quietly and saying, 'Henry, we'll kill each other. We seem to bring out all the very worst qualities in each other. I do all I can and yet you both make me feel like an intruder.'

'It's just your imagination, Martha. Now stop worrying.'

'I'm an unhappy woman. But I try to be patient. I try so hard, don't I, Henry?'

'You're very patient, dear, but you shouldn't be so suspicious of everyone and everybody, don't you see?' Mr Lount was saying in the soothing voice of a man trying to pacify an angry and hysterical wife.

Then Michael heard footsteps on the cinder path, and then he saw two long shadows flung across the road: two women were approaching, and one was a tall, slender girl. When Michael saw this girl, Helen Murray, he tried to duck behind the veranda post, for he had always wanted her for his girl. He had gone to school with her. At night-time he used to lie awake planning remarkable feats that would so impress her she would never want to be far away from him. Now the girl's mother was calling, 'Hello there, Michael,' in a very jolly voice.

'Hello, Mrs Murray,' he said glumly, for he was sure his father's or his mother's voice would rise again.

'Come on and walk home with us, Michael,' Helen called. Her voice sounded so soft and her face in the dusk light seemed so round, white and mysteriously far away that Michael began to ache with eagerness. Yet he said hurriedly, 'I can't. I can't tonight,' speaking almost rudely as if he believed they only wanted to tease him.

As they went on along the path and he watched them, he was really longing for that one bright moment when Helen would pass under the high corner light, though he was thinking with bitterness that he could already hear them talking, hear Mrs Murray saying, 'He's a peculiar boy, but it's not to be wondered at since his father and mother don't get along at all,' and the words were floating up to the verandas of all the houses: inside one of the houses someone had stopped playing a piano, maybe to hear one of the fellows who had been in the lumber-yard that afternoon laughing and telling that young Lount was scared to jump off the roof.

Still watching the corner, Michael suddenly felt that the twisting and pulling in the life in the house was twisting and choking him. 'I'll get out of here. I'll go away,' and he began to think of going to the city. He began to long for freedom in strange places where everything was new and fresh and mysterious. His heart began to beat heavily at the thought of this freedom. In the city he had an uncle Joe who sailed the lake-boats in the summer months and in the winter went all over the south from one race-track to another following the horses. 'I ought to go down to the city tonight and get a job,' he thought: but he did not move; he was still waiting for Helen Murray to pass under the light.

For most of the next day, too, Michael kept to himself. He was up-town once on a message, and he felt like running on the way home. With long sweeping strides he ran steadily on the paths past the shipyard, the church, the railway tracks, his face serious with determination.

But in the late afternoon when he was sitting on the veranda reading, Sammy Schwartz and Ike Hershfield came around to see him. 'Hello Mike, what's new with you?' they said, sitting on the steps very seriously.

'Hello, Sammy, hello, Ike. What's new with you?'

They began to talk to Michael about the coloured* family that had moved into the old roughcast shack down by the tracks. 'The big coon* kid thinks he's tough,' Sammy said. 'He offered to beat up any of us so we said he wouldn't have a snowball's chance* with you.'

'What did the nigger* say?'

'He said he'd pop you one right on the nose if you came over his way.'

'Come on, guys. Let's go over there,' Michael said. 'I'll tear his guts out for you.'

They went out to the street, fell in step very solemnly, and walked over to the field by the tracks without saying a word. When they were about fifty paces away from the shack, Sammy said, 'Wait here. I'll go get the coon,' and he ran on to the unpainted door of the whitewashed house calling, 'Oh, Art, oh, Art, come on out.' A big coloured boy with closely cropped hair came out and put his hand up, shading his eyes from the sun. Then he went back into the house and came out again with a big straw hat on his head. He was in his bare feet. The way he came walking across the field with Sammy was always easy to remember because he hung back a little, talking rapidly, shrugging his shoulders and rolling the whites of his eyes. When he came close to Michael he grinned nervously, flashing his teeth, and said, 'What's the matter with you white boys? I don't want to do no fighting.' He looked scared.

'Come on. Get ready. I'm going to do a nice job on you,' Michael said.

The coloured boy took off his big straw hat and with great care laid it on the ground while all the time he was looking mournfully across the field and at his house, hoping maybe that somebody would come out. Then they started to fight, and Michael knocked him down four times, but he, himself, got a black eye and a cut lip. The coloured boy had been so brave and he seemed so alone, licked and lying on the ground, that they sat down around him, praising him, making friends with him and gradually finding out that he was a good ball player, a left-handed pitcher* who specialized in a curve ball*, and they agreed they could use him, maybe, on the town team.

Lying there in the field, flat on his back, Michael liked it so much that he almost did not want to go away. Art, the coloured boy, was telling how he had always wanted to be a jockey but had got too big; he had a brother who could make the weight. So Michael began to boast about his Uncle Joe who went around to all the tracks in the winter making and losing money at places like Saratoga, Blue Bonnets and Tia Juana. It was a fine, friendly, eager discussion about far-away places.

It was nearly dinner-time when Michael got home; he went in the house sucking his cut lip and hoping his mother would not notice his black eye. But he heard no movement in the house. In the kitchen he saw his stepmother kneeling down in the middle of the floor with her hands clasped and her lips moving.

'What's the matter, Mother?' he asked.

'I'm praying,' she said.

'What for?'

'For your father. Get down and pray with me.'

'I don't want to pray, Mother.'

'You've got to,' she said.

'My lip's all cut. It's bleeding. I can't do it,' he said.

Late afternoon sunshine coming through the kitchen window shone on his stepmother's graying hair, on her soft smooth skin and on the gentle, patient expression that was on her face. At that moment Michael thought that she was desperately uneasy and terribly alone, and he felt sorry for her even while he was rushing out of the back door.

He saw his father walking toward the woodshed, walking slow and upright with his hands held straight at his side and with the same afternoon sunlight shining so brightly on the high dome of his forehead. He went right into the woodshed without looking back. Michael sat down on the steps and waited. He was afraid to follow. Maybe it was because of the way his father was walking with his head held up and his hands straight at his sides. Michael began to make a small desperate prayer that his father should suddenly appear at the woodshed door.

Time dragged slowly. A few doors away Mrs McCutcheon was feeding her hens who were clucking as she called them. 'I can't sit here till it gets dark,' Michael was thinking, but he was afraid to go into the woodshed and afraid to think of what he feared.

So he waited till he could not keep a picture of the interior of the shed out of his thoughts, a picture that included his father walking in with his hands as though strapped at his sides and his head stiff, like a man they were going to hang.

'What's he doing in there, what's he doing?' Michael said out loud, and he jumped up and rushed to the shed and flung the door wide.

His father was sitting on a pile of wood with his head on his hands and a kind of beaten look on his face. Still scared, Michael called out, 'Dad, Dad,' and then he felt such relief he sank down on the pile of wood beside his father and looked up at him.

'What's the matter with you, son?'

'Nothing. I guess I just wondered where you were.'

'What are you upset about?'

'I've been running. I feel all right.'

So they sat there quietly till it seemed time to go into the house. No one said anything. No one noticed Michael's black eye or his cut lip.

Even after they had eaten Michael could not get rid of the fear within him, a fear of something impending. In a way he felt that he ought to do something at once, but he seemed unable to move; it was like sitting on the edge of the roof yesterday, afraid to make the jump. So he went back of the house and sat on the stoop and for a long time looked at the shed till he grew even more uneasy. He heard the angry drilling of a woodpecker and the quiet rippling of the little water flowing under the street bridge and flowing on down over the rocks into the glen. Heavy clouds were sweeping up from the horizon.

He knew now that he wanted to run away, that he could not stay there any longer, only he couldn't make up his mind to go. Within him was that same breathless feeling he had had when he sat on the roof staring down, trying to move. Now he walked around to the front of the house and kept going along the path as far as Helen Murray's house. After going around to the back door, he stood for a long time staring at the lighted window, hoping to see Helen's shadow or her body moving against the light. He was breathing deeply and smelling the rich heavy odours from the flower garden. With his head thrust forward he whistled softly.

'Is that you, Michael?' Helen called from the door.

'Come on out, Helen.'

'What do you want?'

'Come on for a walk, will you?'

For a moment she hesitated at the door, then she came toward him, floating in her white organdie party dress over the grass toward him. She was saying, 'I'm dressed to go out. I can't go with you. I'm going down to the dance hall.'

'Who with?'

'Charlie Delaney.'

'Oh, all right,' he said. 'I just thought you might be doing nothing.' As he walked away he called back to her, 'So long, Helen.'

It was then, on the way back to the house, that he felt he had to go away at once. 'I've got to go. I'll die here. I'll write to Dad from the city.'

No one paid any attention to him when he returned to the house. His father and stepmother were sitting quietly in the living-room reading the paper. In his own room he took a little wooden box from the bottom drawer of his dresser and emptied it of twenty dollars and seventy cents, all that he had saved. He listened solemnly for sounds in the house, then he stuffed a clean shirt into his pocket, a comb, and a toothbrush.

Outside he hurried along with his great swinging strides, going past the corner house, on past the long fence and the bridge and the church, and the shipyard, and past the last of the town lights to the highway. He was walking stubbornly with his face looking solemn and dogged. Then he saw the moonlight shining on the hay stacked in the fields, and when he smelled the oats and the richer smell of sweet clover he suddenly felt alive and free. Headlights from cars kept sweeping by and already he was imagining he could see the haze of bright light hanging over the city. His heart began to thump with eagerness. He put out his hand for a lift, feeling full of hope. He looked across the fields at the dark humps, cows standing motionless in the night. Soon someone would stop and pick him up. They would take him among a million new faces, rumbling sounds, and strange smells. He got more excited. His Uncle Joe might get him a job on the boats for the rest of the summer; maybe, too, he might be able to move around with him in the winter. Over and over he kept thinking of places with beautiful names, places like Tia Juana, Woodbine, Saratoga and Blue Bonnets.

Notes

coloured (p147)

> (*old-fashioned* or *offensive*) of a person from a race that does not have white skin; not an appropriate word now, but often used at the time this story was written

coon, nigger (p147)

> (*slang, taboo*) very offensive words for a black person; now very shocking, taboo words, but less so at the time this story was written

snowball's chance (p147)

> short for the idiomatic expression '(not have) a snowball's chance in hell', meaning 'to have no chance at all'

pitcher, curve ball (p148)

> (*American English*) terms in the game of baseball: the player who throws the ball to the batter; and a ball that moves in a curve when it is thrown to the batter

Discussion

1 Are things really as bad as Michael believes, or is he getting everything out of proportion? Do you feel sympathy for him, or irritation? Was running away the best solution for him? If you were a friend of Michael's, what advice would you give him?

2 We see events in the story only from Michael's point of view. How do you think the other characters view him? Give a brief description of Michael, as seen by these characters:
   a) his father
   b) his stepmother
   c) Art the 'coloured' boy
   d) Helen Murray.

3 What did you think of the incident of Michael's fight with Art, the 'coloured' boy? Why did Michael's friends set the fight up? How do you think the author intended us to interpret this fight – as an unpleasant racist attack, as just a bit of boys' fun, or as a kind of initiation ceremony for a new arrival to the neighbourhood?

LANGUAGE FOCUS

1 Michael accuses his friends of being 'yellow'; later, he is afraid that the same charge can be made against him. The association in English between 'yellow' and 'cowardice' is so strong that the colour can stand for the emotion. Is there the same association in your language? Which colours are associated in English with the following emotions or states?
    anger, cold, rage, fear, misery, envy, fury, seasickness, depression, terror, jealousy, inexperience, embarrassment

2 These words from the story are either more frequent in North American English than in British English, or can have different meanings in each variety:
    lumber, stump, vest, freight, swell, loafer, crony, store, kid, licked, stoop, highway

   Match each word above with its near-equivalent in this list of British English words:
    waistcoat, shop, main road, great, timber, friend, porch, idler, dare, young person, beaten, goods

ACTIVITIES

1 Michael plans to write to his father when he gets to the city. What do you think he might say? Will he explain about the rebuff from Helen Murray, or his longing for freedom, and his feeling that 'the twisting and pulling in the life of the house was twisting and choking him'? Write his letter for him.

2 When Michael's father and stepmother find out that Michael has run away, how do you think they react? Are they upset, do they blame each other, do they want him to come home, do they think it will be good for him to stay with Uncle Joe for a bit? Write a short dialogue between them when they first learn the news in a letter from Michael the next day.

3 Read the last paragraph of the story again. Do you feel that the story ends on a note of hope and optimism, or is there an underlying suggestion that Michael's romantic dreams will soon turn to disillusionment? Write a new ending, briefly describing Michael's adventures that summer, to fit your own interpretation of the mood of the story.

QUESTIONS FOR DISCUSSION OR WRITING

1 The children in these stories are all very different. Imagine that you are a school teacher, and write a short report on the personality of each child, describing what you think are their good and their bad points. Are they shy, nervous, aggressive, self-contained, sensible, and so on? Which child would you least like to have in your class? Why?

2 Which of the children in these stories did you feel most sympathy for? Why? Imagine that you could give that child some helpful advice. What would it be?

3 'Parentage is a very important profession, but no test of fitness for it is ever imposed in the interest of the children,' wrote George Bernard Shaw.
   Do you think he has a point? Would it ever be desirable or feasible to impose a 'test of fitness' on people planning to be parents? What would the test be? Do you think any of the parents in these stories could be classed as 'unfit' to be parents? Which ones, and why?

4 In the stories *The End of the Party* and *Next Term, We'll Mash You*, children are shown as being nasty, even cruel to one another. Do you think that is realistic? Can children really be that horrible? What incidents from real life can you think of which would support this view of children?

5 Look again at the stories *Killing Lizards*, *Friends of Miss Reece*, *Secrets*, and perhaps also *The Rocking-Horse Winner*. In these stories we see the child intervening, or attempting to intervene, in the adult world. What do these interventions have in common, if anything? Could any of them be said to be successful? If they are largely failures, do you think this is probably inevitable, because no child can be expected to understand how the adult world operates?

6 These stories show how the child's (or the adolescent's) world is different from that of adults, and in most of the stories we are given the child's point of view. For each story try to describe the difference between child and adult perceptions, and the effect such differences have. For example,

in *The End of the Party*, the gulf between the two viewpoints leads to tragedy; whereas at the other end of the scale, in *The Open Window*, the difference leads to entertaining confusion.

7   Which story, in your opinion, created the most accurate or believable childhood world? How do you think the author achieved this? Choose the story that you like best, or think is the most effective, and write a short review of it for a newspaper or a magazine.

8   Would any of the stories in this volume make a good short film? Choose one, and write a description of the kind of film you would make. If it is a story told from the point of view of the child, as in *Friends of Miss Reece* or *Secrets*, would you try to convey that viewpoint in the film? How? Would you, for example, shoot a lot of the scenes at a child's eye level? Would you use language appropriate for a child, or would you use a 'voice-over', as though from the child when grown up? What dangers are there in presenting the viewpoint of a child in a film?

Fiction by well-known authors, both classic and modern.
Texts are not abridged or simplified in any way, but have
notes and questions to help the reader.

FROM THE CRADLE
TO THE GRAVE

Editor: Clare West

Short stories by

Evelyn Waugh, Somerset Maugham, Roald Dahl,
Saki, Frank Sargeson, Raymond Carver,
H. E. Bates, Susan Hill

This collection of short stories explores the trials of life from
youth to old age: the idealism of young people, the stresses
and strains of marriage, the anxieties of parenthood, and
the loneliness and fears of older people. The wide variety
of writing styles includes black humour, satire, and
compassionate and realistic observation of the follies and
foibles of humankind.

CRIME NEVER PAYS

Editor: Clare West

Short stories by

*Agatha Christie, Graham Greene,
Ruth Rendell, Angela Noel, Dorothy L. Sayers,
Margery Allingham, Sir Arthur Conan Doyle,
Patricia Highsmith*

Murder: the unlawful, intentional killing of a human being
– a terrible crime. But murder stories are always fascinating.
Who did it? And how? Or why? Was it murder at all, or just
an unfortunate accident? Who will triumph, the murderer
or the detective? This collection contains a wide range of
murder stories, from the astute detection of the famous
Sherlock Holmes, to the chilling psychology of Ruth
Rendell.

A Window
on the Universe

Editor: Jennifer Bassett

Short stories by

Ray Bradbury, Bill Brown, Philip K. Dick,
Arthur C. Clarke, Jerome Bixby, Isaac Asimov,
Brian Aldiss, John Wyndham, Roald Dahl

What does the future hold in store for the human race?
Aliens from distant galaxies, telepathic horror, interstellar
war, time-warps, the shriek of a rose, collision with an
asteroid – the unknown lies around every corner, and the
universe is a big place. These nine science-fiction stories offer
possibilities that are fantastic, humorous, alarming, but
always thought-provoking.

AND ALL FOR LOVE . . .

Editors: Diane Mowat & Jennifer Bassett

Short stories by

Maeve Binchy, Edith Wharton, Virginia Woolf,
James Joyce, H. E. Bates, Grahame Greene,
Fay Weldon, Patricia Highsmith,
John Morrison, Somerset Maugham

What sad, appalling, and surprising things people do in the name of love, and for the sake of love. These short stories give us love won and love lost, love revenged, love thrown away, love in triumph, love in despair. It might be love between men and women, children and parents, even humans and cats; but whichever it is, love is a force to be reckoned with.